This bicentennial anniversary edition of reworked English translation was made available thanks to the previous English and Japanese translations of Captain P. I. Rikord's recollection of his voyages to Japan between 1811 and 1813. The purpose of this edition is to promote contemporary comprehension of these events, an especially important goal in today's global environment. It is our sincere belief that Captain Rikord would desire the wisdom and the friendship that once existed between Russia and Japan and he would want to further improve the relationship between these two countries today.

Lin Sho Doh

麟　勝　堂

admin@LinShoDoh.com

Cover (Japanese brush painting):

This painting was drawn by Denjuro Matsuda (松田伝十郎), author of Hokuidan (北夷談), who was in charge of the escort team for Capt. Golownin and his crew from Matsumae to Hakodate under the Tokugawa Bakufu regime (徳川幕府政権). He also surveyed North Sakhalin with Rinzo Mamiya (間宮林蔵) in 1808 when they achieved discovery of the first safe passage, named Mamiya Strait by Seibold in 1832.

References

Rikord, P.I. *Rikord's Account of His Negotiations with the Japanese*

　London:　Henry Colburn and Co.,　1824

Golownin, W.M. *Memories of a Captivity in Japan 1811-1813*

　Londodn:　Henry Colburn and Co.,　1824

Matsuda, Denjuro　松田伝十郎 (1769-1843)　「北夷談」 *Hokuidan*

　- Japanese National Archives -

Saito, Tomoyuki　斉藤智之　「対日折衝記」 *Tainichi Settsusho Ki*

　Takataya-Kahei Memorial Hall Curator

Takataya-Kahei Memorial Hall Archives 高田屋顕彰館・歴史文化

　資料館　Sumoto-shi, Japan

Hakodate Central Library 函館市中央図書館　Hakodate-shi, Japan

Yushima Sei Doh 湯島聖堂 公益財団法人　斯文会　Tokyo, Japan

Contents

Map (A)

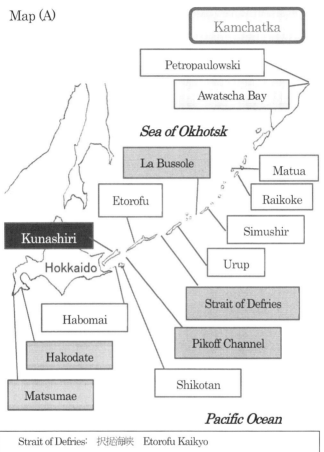

Kamchatka

Petropaulowski

Awatscha Bay

Sea of Okhotsk

La Bussole

Matua

Raikoke

Etorofu

Simushir

Kunashiri

Urup

Hokkaido

Strait of Defries

Habomai

Pikoff Channel

Hakodate

Shikotan

Matsumae

Pacific Ocean

Strait of Defries:　択捉海峡　Etorofu Kaikyo

Pikoff Channel:　国後水道　Kunashiri Suidou

Hakodate → Kunashiri：　about **420km　(263miles)**

Hakodate →Matsumae：　about 48km (30 miles)

Map (B)

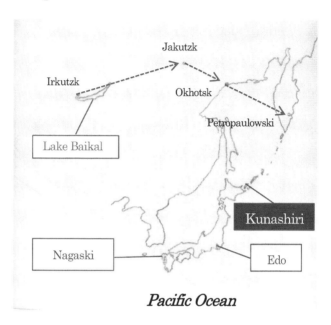

Irkutzk → Jakutzk : about 1,920km (1,200 miles)

Jakutzk → Okhotsk : about 1080km (675 miles)

Okhotsk → Petropaulowski : about 1,296km (810 miles)

Edo → Kunashiri : **about 1,000km (625miles)**

Edo → Nagasaki : **about 1,000km (625miles)**

P.I. Rikord
1776-1855
captain and
author

Takataya-Kahei
1769-1827
merchant and
ship- owner

5

W.M. Golownin

1776-1831

captain and author

Ranks of the Imperial Russian Navy	
General Admiral	Lieutenant
Admiral	Under-Lieutenant
Vice Admiral	Ship Secretary
Rear Admiral	Midshipman
Captain-Commodore	Stuurman
Captain, 1st rank	Skipper
Captain, 2nd rank	Midshipman
Captain, 3rd rank	Boatsman

— The First Voyage —

It was on July 11, 1811, at eleven o'clock in the morning that the melancholy incident took place. This was also in the eleventh month of the year, according to the ancient calendar. For all who served on the sloop *Diana*, it reminded a painful recollection never to be erased from our memory.

An unexpected misfortune fell upon Captain Golownin that filled us with anxiety and disappointment, and demolished the hope of a speedy return to our country that we talked about when we leave Kamchatka. But fate cruelly separated us from our worthy and beloved captain, who had been for five years our constant companion in danger. We lost all hope of seeing our relatives and friends again, and turned to the mighty God for protection. Officers and seamen of the *Diana* unanimously determined not to leave the coasts of Japan until all possible efforts were made to retrieve their comrades, if they were still alive or to avenge them if they were dead.

We had followed the progress of Captain Golownin and his escorts from the ship to the gate of the fortress with our telescopes. We had observed a great number of men dressed in brilliant and various colors and supposed those could be Japanese officers. As they had followed Captain Golownin's arrangements, I had no suspicions of treachery by the Japanese. Indeed, I so blindly relied on their sincerity that I even prepared a festive reception for the strangers.

I thought it probable that our Captain would invite some of the Japanese officers to come on board with him. Toward noon, while preparations were still in progress, we suddenly heard reports of muskets and frightful screams on the shore. We saw a large number of people rush out of the fortress gate, and run toward the boat where Captain Golownin landed. We could clearly distinguish by our telescope that these people hastened without any orders, and they took possessions of the mast, the sail, the rudder, and all the riggings of the boat. We could also perceive them dragging one of the crewmen and the Kurile, into the fortress through the gate, which was closed soon after.

Instantly a profound stillness prevailed. The buildings stood nearly to the sea and were draped with stripped cotton cloth. We were thus prevented from observing what had passed behind this curtain, and no one appeared in front of it. We were completely shut off from the fate of our comrades. Those people who are acquainted with <u>Japanese history</u> can well anticipate what we had to expect from the vindictive character of the people.

Without much delay, I gave an order for weighing anchor, and advanced toward the village. I expected that the Japanese would perhaps abandon their intention on perceiving our sloop of war near them and hoped to enter into negotiation to release our comrades. But we were compelled to cast anchor at a tolerable distance from the land as the depth of the water suddenly diminished to <u>two and half fathoms</u>. We were near enough to make our shots reach the works, but too far off to cause any damage. As we were preparing for action, the Japanese also opened their batteries on the heights, but their shots passed over us.

The honor of my country and our flag respected by all civilized powers, were thus grossly insulted, and I determined to fire upon the place. We fired about one hundred and seventy guns, and observed that our shots reached the batteries, but without producing any significant result. The whole works toward the sea were surrounded by a very thick earthen bank. However, we experienced little damages from the enemy's fire. As it was unnecessary to remain longer in this situation, we ceased fire, and weighed anchor. The Japanese then became bolder, and fired even more fiercely as we receded from the village. As I did not have a sufficient number of men to venture landing, I could undertake nothing decisively for the rescue of our comrades. We were only fifty-one men including officers. We had lost our beloved and honored captain, who in traversing the ocean had watched over us with anxious care through many difficulties. And now treachery snatched our bravest captain Golownin from us, who probably experienced the cruelest fate. These reflections exasperated the whole crew to the highest degree.

They all desired to retaliate for the perfidy of the Japanese, and were all ready to storm the fortress, and execute dreadful charges, even at the risk of all their lives. With such men, animated with these feelings, it would not be difficult to inflict serious consequences on the enemy.

But for such an endeavor, the ship must be left unprotected, and it might be easily set on fire. Then the success of our attempt may never be known in Russia, and all the observations, which we collected during our voyage in the Kurile Islands, could be lost. Therefore, we weighed anchor out of guns range from the fortress, and determined to write to our beloved captain. In our letter we expressed our grief for his capture, and our indignation at the conduct of Kunashiri governor, whose aggression was a direct infringement of the law-abiding nations. We informed him that we would return immediately to <u>Okhotsk</u>, to report what had happened, but we were at the same time all prepared to risk our lives for release. All the officers signed this letter, and it was deposited in a cask which was placed near the harbor. Toward evening we moved from the shore, and held ourselves in readiness for the night, in case of an enemy attack.

Next morning we observed by our telescope that the Japanese were removing their possessions on packhorses, probably with the idea that we intended to set fire to the village. At eight o'clock in the morning, as a deputy captain I assumed the command of the ship with the most painful feelings, and requested all the officers to state in writing the best means we could resort to for the release of our comrades.

They all concurred it would be preferable to discontinue hostilities that could have no useful result, and might cause a worse fate for the prisoners. And it was decided to return to Okhotsk, and to obtain sufficient means from our government, either for release of our unfortunate comrades or as the case may be, for avenging their death.

When it was daylight, I sent the <u>second pilot</u>, Srednago to the cask by boat, for the purpose of seeing whether or not the letter we placed in it the day before had been removed. But before he reached the cask, he heard drums beating within the fortress, and he quickly returned for fear of being captured by the Japanese <u>baidare</u>. We soon observed a baidare advancing from the shore. After coming a short distance, they tossed out a new cask with a black pennant. We weighed anchor, stood into the harbor and manned a boat for the purpose of examining whether the cask contained a letter or any information on our comrades.

However, we perceived that the cask was attached to a rope at the other end, which was stretched to the shore. It was imperceptibly drawn shoreward, enticing our boat near to the land with the intent to eventually capture it. We once more cast the anchor, and we were again plunged into all the torments of incertitude. Yet, it was still unknown whether our comrades had become victims of the sanguinary spirit of Asiatic vengeance, or whether the prudence of the Japanese restrained them from sacrificing seven helpless prisoners.

The only thing left for us to do then was to make it appear that we did not doubt the continued existence of our unfortunate comrades, and that we considered the Japanese incapable of treating prisoners in a manner inconsistent with the practice of civilized powers. With this view I dispatched <u>Midshipman</u> Filatoff to the promontory in a boat with the officers' linen, razors, and books, and the clothes of sailors, all well packed up. This packet bore a superscription with orders to leave these items in the deserted village.

On the fourteenth, we left this bay with painful feelings. The officers of the *Diana* appropriately named it THE BAY OF DECEIT, and set the rudder-wheel to Okhotsk. A persistent thick fog was all we had to complain of during the voyage. All other conditions including the wind were favorable and moderate. But the storm in my soul raged with unbounded fury for the few days that Kunashiri Island was in our sight, despite the calm wind.

However, a feeble ray of hope sometimes cheered us that we were not for ever separated from our comrades. I observed the coast from morning to night through a telescope in the hope of perceiving someone who might have escaped in a boat. When we reached the eastern ocean where the fog scarcely permitted us to see a few fathoms around us, a most gloomy reflection tormented me, and allowed me no repose either day or night. We inhabited the same cabin which we had shared for five years with Captain Golownin and the cabin had scarcely changed since the unfortunate day of his capture. It constantly reminded me of his absence.

The officers coming to me with reports frequently addressed me with his name out of habit.

Whenever this occurred, the tears started filling our eyes. How often had I here discussed with him the possibility of reestablishing good understanding with the Japanese after the actions of some imprudent men. How delighted we were at the idea of thus being serviceable to our country! Captain Golownin, two distinguished officers and four sailors were snatched from us by the people who were notorious in Europe for their cruel persecution of Christians. Thus, their fate was enfolded in impenetrable obscurity.

On the sixteenth day of our voyage, the village of Okhotsk began to rise in our view from the sea. The new church was particularly distinguishable and attractive to us, especially for those who had been deprived of the consolation of seeing a church for a long time. The sight of a Christian church was always a comfort to the eyes of a sailor, even more so to those who struggled with misfortune. Favorable ideas about the inhabitants were awakened by the sight of the church at new landing places. Here the low promontory, or rather the sandbank on which Okhotsk is built, was not descried in approaching it from the sea until the whole village was seen at once.

In order to lose no time I ordered a signal to be made by hoisting a flag, and firing a gun, and waited for a pilot. The commandant of the port soon sent out Lieutenant Schachoff with directions to the best anchoring ground. I immediately reported to the commandant of the port, Captain Minitzky, the misfortune which had fallen upon Captain Golownin. Captain Golownin was bound to Captain Minitzky as well as to me by ties of friendship, ever since we all served together in the English fleet. Captain Minitzky shared my feelings most sincerely. I am indebted to him for his prudent advice, and active cooperation Indeed, had it not been for him, the highest authority might have concluded, from the unstudied manner in which I had drawn up my report that I did not make every possible effort which duty required for the release of Captain Golownin.

As my stay in Okhotsk during the winter could be of no advantages to the public service, I proceeded to Irkutzk with consent of Captain Minitzky, intending to continue to Petersburg. My purpose was to inform the Minister of Marine of every particular that had occurred, and to receive his order regarding a fresh voyage to the Japanese coasts for the liberation of our comrades. Thus after fulfilling our government orders and collecting information on remote countries, we terminated a voyage, which had cost us many sacrifices. We had undertaken this voyage with the consoling persuasion we should return again to the bosoms of our families, but the hard fate which struck our comrades had demolished this hope.

It was necessary that I should complete the journey to Petersburg, and travel back to Okhotsk in the same winter. I could not therefore wait to go by the sledge-road from Jakutzk, where I arrived at the end of September. I was obliged to travel on horseback to Irkutzk, and accomplished the whole distance of three thousand wersts in fifty-six days. This single journey by land was more exhausting to me than all my sea voyages. The vertical jolting of a horse was a real torment to sailors who were only accustomed to the motion of the waves.

In order to gain time, sometimes I ventured to ride two long stretches each of forty-five wersts in twenty-four hours. I felt as if my whole body had been broken apart on a wheel, and even my jaws refused to correctly function.

The autumn road from Jakutzk to Irkutzk, is very dangerous when traveled only on horseback. It consists of many narrow paths, passing along steep declivities that form the banks of the Lena. In many places the streams are vaulted over with pieces of ice, which the inhabitants call "nakips." And, as the Jakutzkan horses are generally unshod, they often slip on the ice.

One time as I was riding tolerably fast, without perceiving a dangerous nakip, I fell very suddenly failing to extricate my foot from the stirrup, and I rolled down the precipice together with my horse. I had to pay the price for this fall with a sprained ankle, but I wanted to thank for the God that I did not break my neck. I would therefore advise those who travel such roads, not to allow distracting thoughts while on the horse. Horses have a bad habit of climbing up the precipices when they meet with a nakip on an abrupt declivity. The slippery fall is almost inevitable.

In Irkutzk I was very kindly received by the Civil Governor Treskin, whom I met since the governor general of Siberia was out of the office. My account from the commandant of Okhotsk was already received and it had been long since forwarded to the superior authorities in Petersburg, together with a request for the new expedition to the Japanese coasts for the liberation of the prisoners.

This was unexpected, but certainly it was a very gratifying situation since it was solely for the sake of this voyage that I had made the dangerous journey from Okhotsk to Petersburg. I now needed to await the approbation of the governor in Irkutzk for the final decision on the subject. Civil Governor Treskin displayed great sorrow for Captain Golownin's misfortune, and assisted me in drawing up the plan of the expedition, which was immediately forwarded to Governor General Pestel for his inspection.

However, because of the political pressure at that period, the sanction of the Emperor was not obtainable, and I received an order to return to Okhotsk. We proceeded to complete our unfinished survey on the sloop *Diana* with the permission of the proper authorities, and also to visit Kunashiri Island in order to find out the fate of our comrades.

During the winter, <u>Leonsaimon</u> who was already acquainted with *"Captain Golownin's Narrative"* was brought to Irkutzk by the express command of the civil governor. It took great pains to convince him of the amicable intention of our government but we apparently succeeded. He understood Russian tolerably well, and he assured us that the Russians would be taken care of in Japan, and that the investigation by his government would be brought to a happy conclusion soon.

With this Japanese company, I returned to Okhotsk not on horseback as before, but in a convenient winter-carriage along the frozen Lena, as far as Jakutzk where we took our departure at the end of March. The spring blossoms began at this season of the year in the country, which was blessed with the smiles of nature but here winter was so severe that pieces of ice still served the poor inhabitants as windows, and were not yet exchanged for Muscovy glass as happens when the thaw sets in.

The road to Okhotsk was so deeply covered with snow that it was impassable for horses. Neither I nor my Japanese companion had the patience to wait for the snow to melt. We seated ourselves on rein-deer, and their masters, tough Tungusians, were our conductors. I must say these beautiful and useful animals are much more convenient for riding in these countries than horses are. They do not plunge, and are so tame in case of falling, that they stand still as if they were fixed to the ground. We learned this frequently on the first day of our journey. We experienced many falls, due to the kind of saddles used on reindeer, and the manner in which they were placed. These saddles are very small and unsteady. They have no stirrups, and they are placed upon the shoulders of the reindeer, which have backs too weak to bear any weight.

On my arrival in Okhotsk, I found the *Diana* already stocked with the most necessary supplies. But, it was impossible to immediately procure everything needed for her voyage, because of the great inconveniences which the river Ochota presented. Despite these difficulties we finally succeeded, thanks to Captain Minitzky getting the ship in as good condition as if it has been prepared in the best

Russian port. I therefore publicly gave him appreciation for his great contribution to the success of my voyage.

To increase the number of the *Diana's* crew, he gave me a non-commissioned officer and ten men of the Okhotsk corps of marines. And to diminish the danger of the voyage, he arranged for an Okhotsk transport brig named the *Sotik* to accompany us. For the command of this I appointed one of my officers, Lieutenant Filatoff. I also selected Lieutenant Jakuschkin for the command of another transport, called the *Paul*. Both were bound to Kamchatka.

On July 18, 1812, when everything was completed for departure, I received six Japanese into our ship who had been shipwrecked on the coasts of Kamchatka, and whom I wished to return to their country. These men deserve to be mentioned along with the shipwreck incident. It happened during the same year our comrades were captured on the Japanese coast. It seemed God had purposely arranged it so that the number of detained Japanese was equal to that of our comrades in Japan. According to European views, an exchange should have easily been made, but Japanese laws and our laws turned out to be much different in reality.

About three o'clock in the afternoon, on July 22, we set sail together with the brig *Sotik*. My intention was to take the shortest distance to Kunashiri Island by the either <u>Pikoff Channel</u>, or at least by the <u>Strait of Defries</u>.

Nothing worthy of remark occurred on this voyage except one great danger we were in. On July 27, about mid-day, the clouded sky was so cleared that we were able to determine our location with considerable accuracy. We were thirty-seven miles northward of St. John Island which had been discovered by Billings in the ship *Russia's Glory* on a voyage from Okhotsk to Kamchatka. Its geographical location was very correctly determined by Captain Krusenstern through astronomical observation.

In general, all the marine locations determined could serve for the regulation of the chronometer with as much accuracy as the observatory at Greenwich. Therefore, we had no doubts concerning our location relative to this island, particularly as we had used the meridian altitude of the sun very correctly on the same day.

We then determined to adjust our direction to pass the island at the distance of ten miles, and I signaled to the *Sotik* to keep within about half a mile astern of the *Diana*. I wished if the weather should permit, to make observations on St. John, because it lies out of the usual course from Okhotsk to Kamchatka and is therefore very seldom seen either by the company's ship or by the Okhotsk transports.

On July 28 at midnight, we had a breeze accompanied by thick fog, and about two o'clock in the morning we suddenly perceived a high rock straight ahead of the ship and scarcely <u>twenty fathoms</u> distant. It was indeed a dreadful situation. We were in the midst of the ocean with a perpendicular rock so near, that every moment we expected the ship to be shattered into pieces. Who could conceive our deliverance possible?   God, however, protected us.

We instantly endeavored to put about and checked the vessel course rapidly if we could not entirely avoid the danger. To minimize the damage we had to at least avoid contact with the rock. We felt only some slight shocks on the bows, and perceived open passage toward the south. There were rocks on every side. We directed our course through them. Ultimately, we were fortunate to clear the rocks which threatened us with destruction, but we descried others through the mist.   After struggling at this passage we followed the current, and succeeded in getting through another strait also formed by frightful rocks. Leaving behind these threatening rocks in the distance, we warned the *Sotik* of the approaching danger by fog-signal. She also fortunately avoided destruction.

The fog dispersed at about four o'clock and

we perceived the whole extent of the danger which we had passed through. St. John was scarcely visible within the surrounding rocks. It was about a mile in circumference, and had less the appearance of an island than of conical form rocks, and it was inaccessible from all sides. Near to it on the east, there were four large rocks and the current conveyed us between them. We did not observe these rocks at first because of the thick fog. The view of these rocks now reminded us of our terror and it was greater than what we had experienced during the previous dreadful night. We were so eagerly working on the ship that we had no time to reflect on the ultimate terror which seemed to be awaiting us.

We passed the rocks so near that we could have become stranded upon them. The sloop struck them three times and every strike shrank my soul. Our voices were completely drowned by the roaring waves. None of my orders could be heard. Despair crossed my heart, along with regret that the six Japanese we depended on for the release of our comrades were now about to perish. But then the weather cleared up, and to our joy we saw our *Sotik* beside St. John at a short distance. But the atmosphere soon turned much fogger than ever, and prevented us from seeing more than a few fathoms around us.

Nothing remarkable happened after this. Contrary winds are not extra ordinary difficulties in voyages. About three o'clock in the afternoon on August 12, we saw the first land, which was the north end of <u>Urup Island</u>, but because of the fog and unfavorable wind we could not pass Defries Strait until August 15.

The same difficulties detained us thirteen days on the coasts of <u>Etorofu</u>, <u>Shikotan</u> and Kunashiri, so that we did not arrive at the place which we had a year before named the Bay of Deceit until August 28.

As we passed the works at gun-shot distance, we observed a new battery of fourteen cannons erected in two tiers, one above the other. As soon as we appeared in the bay, the Japanese concealed themselves. They did not fire, nor we could perceive any movement whatsoever in the place. All the buildings toward the shore were draped with striped cotton cloth, so that we could only see the roof of the large barracks. All their boats were moored on the shore. Since they did not fire, we began to hope that the Japanese were now more favorable toward us than they had been last time. We anchored at two miles distance from the works.

It was already mentioned that Leonsaimon, one of the native Japanese on our ship, understood some Russian. He had been carried away six years ago by Lieutenant Chwostoff. We proposed to write a short letter to the governor of the island with his assistance, extracting from a memorandum which the civil governor of Irkutzk had written. It stated the reason that our government sent the *Diana* to the Japanese coast, and after describing the treachery practiced against Captain Golownin, it concluded in the following terms:

Despite this unexpected hostile act, we are bound to fulfill the commands of our Emperor, and to send back all the Japanese who were shipwrecked on the coasts of Kamchatka; whereby it is obvious that we do not entertain any kind of hostile intention, and we persuade ourselves that the Russian prisoners will also be restored to us as innocent persons, who have harmed no one. But if, contrary to our expectations such liberation cannot take place, in consequence of its being necessary to await the decision of the Japanese government, or on account of other circumstances, we will return next year with the same request.

In the translation of this letter, Leonsaimon in whom we placed all of our hopes betrayed us to practice some deception. A few days before our arrival in Kunashiri, I asked him to write a translation, but he constantly pretended the letter was too diffuse, and he did not translate it. He said in his broken Russian,

25

"I translate what you say and I will write a short letter. With us letter must not be long. We do not love the compliment but the thing; —Chinese writes so to us and lose all the sense."

In consequence of this Japanese style, I had no choices but let him do it in his own way. On the day of our arrival at Kunashiri, I called him into the cabin and requested the letter. He gave it to me on half a sheet of paper which was entirely excessive. In his hieroglyphic mode of writing, a single character sometimes expressed a sentence, so that half-sheet probably contained a very circumstantial description of all that he considered necessary to communicate to his government. It might prove very disadvantageous to the settlement.

I told him the letter appeared much too long for my objective. Without a doubt, he had included a great deal related solely to his own affairs. So, I asked him, if he had no objections, to read it to me in Russian. He did not seem in the least offended at this request but told me the paper contained in fact three letters. The first was short and explained our business, the second contained an account of the Japanese shipwreck, and the third gave a description of the misfortunes he himself had experienced in Russia. I told him that it was only necessary to send the first letter at present, and the others must be deferred until another opportunity. But if he was desirous to send all three together he must give me their copies. He immediately copied the first without hesitation, but stopped at the others, saying they were too difficult.

I said, *"How can they be too difficult, since you wrote them yourself?"* He answered angrily, *"I will sooner destroy them."* He immediately took up a penknife, cut off part of the paper and put it in his mouth. After chewing it for a few moments with a cunning and spiteful expression, he swallowed it in my presence. Thus, the contents of the paper remained mystery. But what we regretted above all, was that we had to rely on this malignant and artful wretch! I now wished to find out whether he had actually written our business on the remaining pieces of the paper. During our voyage, I had frequently discussed on many circumstances with him regarding Japan, and noted down the Japanese translations of a great number of Russian words. I also out of mere curiosity made him try to pronounce and write several Russian family names. Of course, that of my unfortunate friend Wassili Michailowitsch Golownin was not omitted.

I now requested him to show me the place in the letter where this name stood. He did so, and I compared the characters with those I already had.

And I convinced myself the letter really indicated Golownin. Then, I commissioned one of our Japanese to deliver the letter, in person, to the governor of the island. We put him ashore opposite to our anchored place. He was immediately surrounded by hairy Kuriles, who had probably concealed themselves behind the thick tall grass in order to watch us. He accompanied them to the fortress, and he had scarcely approached the gate when the batteries began to fire upon the bay.

These were the first shots discharged since our arrival. I asked Leonsaimon, *"Why did they fire when they saw only a single man from the Russian ship was approaching the village?"* He answered, *"In Japan it is so, such law; they do not kill a man but shoot."*

This unexpected action on the part of the Japanese abolished every hope that I had formed of negotiating with them. At first they did not fire when we approached the fortress, but now they started fire upon our flag of truce.

It was not easy to explain, but it indicated nothing favorable. No movement was made on the ship, and the boat which carried the Japanese to shore had returned and lay alongside. At the gate of the fortress our Japanese was surrounded by a multitude of people, and we soon lost sight of him.

Three days passed without his return.

During the whole of this time, we were constantly occupied from morning to night in viewing the shore through the telescope so as not to miss even the smallest object at the place where the Japanese had landed by the fortress. We often imagined we saw him, and cried out with joy, *"Here comes our messenger!"*

Such deceptions were sometimes of long duration, particularly after sunset and in foggy weather. When the light refraction so wonderfully increased size of objects, we often mistook a crow with extended wings for the Japanese in his loose night-gown. Leonsaimon himself frequently stood several hours together with the telescope in his hands, and seemed much surprised that nobody came to us. The fortress remained closed as a tomb.

As night approached, we always prepared the ship for action in case of attack. A deep silence prevailed, and was only disturbed by the echo of the watch-word of our sentinels. This resounded through-out the bay, and informed our enemy that we were not slumbering. As we were in need of fresh water, I ordered a boat to put ashore with armed men for the purpose of filling our water casks. One of the Japanese was dispatched on the same boat to explain to the governor why the Russian ships had come to these coasts. I asked Leonsaimon to send a short memo with him, but he declined, saying, *"As no answer is made to the first letter, I fear to write again in contradiction to our laws."*

He advised me, however, to draw up a memorandum in the Russian language, which the Japanese who bore it, might translate. I did so. In the course of a few hours this second messenger returned, saying that he had been admitted to the governor and presented the paper I wrote. However, the governor did not take it. Our messenger then told the governor that the Russians had sent some men on shore to get water. He said, *"Very well, let them take water. And as for you, go back where you came from."* and he left without another word. Our Japanese spent some time among a number of hairy Kuriles but as he did not understand their language, he learned nothing from them. He told us that the Japanese remained at a distance, and did not venture to approach him. Finally, the Kuriles turned him out of the fortress gate by force. The honest fellow told me that he wished to remain on the land, and he begged the governor with tears in his eyes to allow him to stay at least one night, but he was refused. We therefore concluded that our first messenger had met with the same reception, and with a fear of experiencing no better treatment from us, as he brought no news of our comrades, he had concealed himself among the hills, or perhaps had gone to some other village on the island.

I wished on a subsequent day to provide us with more water, and for that purpose sent the remaining empty casks to shore at about four o'clock in the afternoon. The Japanese who attentively watched all our motions began to fire at random, though our boats were already near the shore. In order to avoid the hostilities, I recalled the boats by signals, and the Japanese immediately ceased firing. We had been here in the Bay of Deceit for seven days, and it was evident that the commandant's decided distrust of our intentions prevailed. Either due to his own reluctance, or possibly by order of his government, he refused any communications with us. How then could we hope to hear about our comrades?

We recollected several articles belonging to our unhappy friends that we had left in a fishing village in the previous year, and we wished to ascertain whether they were carried away. Accordingly Lieutenant Filatoff commanded the brig to land and visit the village, accompanied by a party of armed men. Firing commenced from the batteries when the brig approached the shore. However, because of the great distance, it proved ineffective. After a few hours elapsed, Lieutenant Filatoff informed me that the house in the fishing village where the articles were left was quite empty. This made it seem that the situation was favorable to us and our comrades were still in existence.

On the following day I sent the same Japanese ashore again, to inform the commandant why the landing was made by the brig. I prevailed upon Leonsaimon, with considerable difficulties, to translate a short memo into Japanese in which I requested the governor to grant me an interview. I wished likewise to state my reason for sending the brig to the fishing village, but the obstinate Leonsaimon refused to make this explanation. The Japanese returned early on the following morning. The governor had received the letter, but instead of returning a written answer, he merely said, *"Well, well, the Russian captain may hold an interview with me in the city."*

This led me to return a decided refusal. It would have been absurd for me to accept the invitation to the city. As regarded our reason for landing at the fishing-village, the governor observed,

"What things? They were taken away immediately." This equivocal answer once more gave us reason to fear that our unfortunate friends were no longer in existence. Besides, our Japanese messenger was not suffered to pass the night in the village, and had no choices but to spend the night on the grass near the

shore, opposite from the *Diana*. To carry on further correspondence by means of Japanese appeared perfectly useless with people who understood not a word of Russian.

So far, we had received no written answer to any of our letters, and therefore we were harassed by a most tormenting uncertainty. We did not wish to dispatch Leonsaimon to the commandant of the island except in a case of most urgent necessity, lest he should be forcibly detained or feel reluctant to return, as he was the only interpreter who understood Russian.

Therefore, I thought of another scheme. It appeared that without any violation of our pacific conduct toward the Japanese, we might stop one of the vessels which we frequently observed sailing near us, and thus endeavor to communicate with someone. Then, we might obtain more information about our comrades. In this way we expected to release ourselves from our difficulties, and avoid another unnecessary voyage to Kunashiri. We anxiously watched for three days, but no ships appeared within our sight, and we concluded that the Japanese had suspended their navigation as autumn had already set in. Our only hope rested now on Leonsaimon.

I wished if possible to ascertain his real sentiments before I sent him on shore. For this purpose I suggested that he writes a letter to his friends, as I intended to depart the next morning. On hearing this, his countenance suddenly changed, and with evident embarrassment he thanked me for the information, saying, *"Well, I will merely write to tell them that they never need expect to see me again."* Then with the most violent agitation he exclaimed, *"I will put an end to my days—will go no more to sea—must die among the Russians!"* To detain a man in such a state of mind could be of very little use to us. It was possible to recognize a cause for this feeling he manifested when we considered the sufferings he bore during his six years of captivity in Russia. There was indeed a reason to fear.

He was bereft of every hope of returning to his native country. He would not fail to commit suicide in a fit of despair. Therefore, I resolved to employ him to lay our propositions once more before the governor, and if possible to convince him to grant me an interview. Being acquainted with my determination, Leonsaimon immediately swore that he will bring me all the information he could collect, and he would return if he was not forcibly detained. As there was at least a possibility that he would not return, it was advisable to adopt the following precautions. I directed that he should be accompanied by his countryman who had already been sent on shore, and I provided Leonsaimon with three cards,

On the first card was written, *"Captain Golownin, and the rest of the Russians are in Kunashiri."*

On the second, *"They have been removed to Matsumae, or Nangasaki, or Edo."* And on the third, *"They are dead."* It was agreed if Leonsaimon were detained, he should give one of these cards to the accompanying Japanese. He could also delete or add such words as the information he should obtain might require.

We sent them ashore on September 4, and to our great joy we saw them both come out of the fortress on the following day. We immediately sent the boat to shore and we were cheered by the hope of hearing new information about our comrades. Meanwhile we watched them closely with our telescope, and to our astonishment, perceived that the other Japanese quitted Leonsaimon, and turned in the opposite direction, concealing himself behind the thick grasses. Leonsaimon came on board the ship alone. On my inquiring where his companion was, he replied that he knew nothing about him. We all thronged to hear his words with eager anxiety, but he requested an interview with me in the cabin.

He then, in the presence of Lieutenant Rudakoff, stated all the difficulties he had experienced in gaining access to the governor before hearing a word the governor inquired, *"Why did the Captain not come on shore himself?"* Leonsaimon replied that he knew nothing about my reason for not doing so, but the objective of his errand was to learn about Captain Golownin and the other Russian prisoners. Harassed between hope and fear, we waited to hear the answer of the governor but Leonsaimon wished first to be assured that no harm would come to him for disclosing the truth. I assured him that he had nothing to fear, and he pronounced the dreadful words: *"They are all dead!"*

This information plunged us into the deepest affliction, and we could not without horror cast our eyes toward the shore where the blood of our comrades was shed. As I had received no instructions on how to act in such a case, it appeared I should be justified in taking vengeance on the faithless Japanese. We were well convinced that our government would never allow their atrocities to pass unpunished.

However, I wished to obtain more certain evidence than the mere words of Leonsaimon, and sent him back again to the fortress with orders to obtain a written confirmation from the commandant. Moreover, we promised immediately to liberate him and the other Japanese we still had on board. At the same time I gave orders for preparing both vessels for action in case we should adopt hostile measures.

Leonsaimon was to return on that day, but we did not see him. The following day likewise elapsed without his appearance. Our expectation of his return was therefore very uncertain. At the same time, his absence left the sad information we had received still subject to a shade of doubt. Therefore, I decided not to leave the bay until we came across a vessel or some individual we could hear the truth from.

On the morning of September 6, we discovered a Japanese baidare. I immediately sent Lieutenant Rudakoff to capture it and placed under his command Srednago and Sawelieff, two officers who had both volunteered on this first hostile campaign. Our boat quickly overtook the baidare, and captured it near the land. The crew immediately jumped over boat, and they scattered to escape.

Two Japanese and a hairy Kurile were found by Mr. Sawelieff where they were concealed among the bushes. Unfortunately we could not obtain any information from them. When I began to interrogate them, they fell on their knees and answered every question with the hissing exclamation, "Sche! Sche!" Every kindness was attempted, but all our endeavors to extract information from them proved fruitless. Heavens! I thought. What method can now be devised to obtain an explanation from these unaccountable people?

On the following morning we saw a large Japanese ship steering toward the harbor. I immediately dispatched Lieutenant Filatoff with express orders not to resort to violence, but merely to terrify the crew and when they surrendered to bring the captain to me. After a few hours, we observed that Lieutenant Filatoff had obtained possession of the Japanese ship, and he was towing it toward our anchoring ground.

On his return, Lieutenant Filatoff made the following report: "When our boats approached the Japanese ship, she seemed to have a great number of armed men on board. She took no notice of being hailed, but continued on her course. We fired some shots toward her in the air. The Japanese immediately slackened sail, and as the ship was close to the shore, several crewmen jumped over, in the hope of escaping by swimming. Those who were near our boat were picked up; the rest either swam ashore or drowned in the sea."

The whole Japanese crew amounted to about sixty individuals, but only the captain was brought to me. His rich yellow dress, his sabre, and other circumstances indicated that he was a man of distinction. I brought him immediately to the cabin. He saluted me according to the Japanese fashion, with demonstrations of high respect. I assured him that he had no cause for alarm, and he sat on a chair in the cabin with great frankness of manner. I then questioned him in Japanese, of which I had learned a little from Leonsaimon.

He told me that his name was <u>Takataya-Kahei,</u> and he had the rank of <u>Sendo-Funamochi</u>, a term which means that he is a commander and owner of several ships. He mentioned that ten belonged entirely to himself. He came from Etorofu Island and was proceeding to the harbor of <u>Hakodate</u> in the territory of the Matsumae clan, with a cargo of dried fish, but contrary winds pushed him into Kunashiri Bay.

In order to explain our actions, I showed him the letter which Leonsaimon had written to the commandant of the island. Having read it, he suddenly exclaimed that Captain Moor and five other Russians are now in the Matsumae. He then informed me when the prisoners were brought from Kunashiri, and also through which villages they were transported, and how long they remained in each place. At the same time he gave me a description of Mr. Moor but he did not mention a word about Captain Golownin. This alone discouraged us. We reflected that in his situation, he might naturally wish to persuade us that our comrades were still alive. Yet, how could he invent the prisoners' circumstances in only a few minutes?

On the other hand, we could not rely on Leonsaimon. What could induce him to fabricate a tale so distressing our feelings? Perhaps revenge for the atrocities committed by Chwostoff on the coasts of Japan? Or was he afraid of being detained on the *Diana*, if he informed us our comrades were alive? But might he not have sent back one of the cards without returning himself? After all, it was possible such a message had really been sent by the governor of the island, so that he might rid himself of all further troubles. Although we were in a state of complete uncertainty, there seemed a probability that our comrades were still alive, and I abandoned all thoughts of hostilities. However, our seamen whose minds were thrown into a state of fermentation by the distressing news were not so easily calmed. Some declared to one officer that they recognized in the government official, the same official they had seen on Etorofu Island in the previous summer, when we held our first conference with the Japanese.

Moor and Novitzky had been present at that conference, and the latter likewise declared that he perceived a striking resemblance between our prisoner and the officer who was on that island. Besides, he recollected perfectly well that the Etorofu official had written down Moor's name. The seamen, who by my orders had assembled on the main deck, then exclaimed that it was not surprising that he knew Moor. But he could give us no information of our beloved Captain Golownin. Our comrades must have perished, and all of us were ready to shed our blood to avenge their treacherous murder. I secretly cherished the same feelings.

I told them that there was still hope that our comrades were alive. But if, they were dead, our government without doubt would give us an opportunity of manifesting our zeal in avenging so foul a crime. From that moment I chose not to engage in any hostile activities until I succeeded bringing Takataya-Kahei to Kamchatka. I was hoping that in the course of the winter, with God's help, we might obtain some positive information regarding our comrades' fate and the views of the Japanese government. Our prisoner seemed to be far superior in rank to any of the Japanese we had so far met. We consequently supposed that he was better acquainted with the affairs of his country. We afterwards learned that he was a very rich merchant and a commander of his own ships; he must have enjoyed, according to the Japanese laws, privileges corresponding with the officers' provisions. Therefore, we decided to call him Natschalnik *(commander or chief)*.

I told him that he must be prepared to accompany me to Russia, and explained the circumstances which compelled me to make such an arrangement. He understood perfectly well, and when I mentioned my belief that Captain Golownin and Moor, and the rest of Russian prisoners must have been put to death, he suddenly interrupted, and exclaimed, *"That is not true! Captain Moor and five Russians are alive in Matsumae where they are well treated, and enjoy the freedom of walking in the city accompanied by two officers."*

When I told him that we intended to take him with us, he replied with astonishing coolness, *"Well, well, I am ready!"* and merely requested that on our arrival in Russia he might continue to live with me. I promised, once he accepted this proposal, that I would send him back to Japan in the ensuing year. He then seemed perfectly reconciled with his unexpected destiny.

The four Japanese who still remained on board the ship understood not a word of Russian. Besides, they were so afflicted with scurvy that they would in all probability have perished if they wintered in Kamchatka. Therefore, I thought it advisable to set them at liberty. Having furnished them with every necessity, I ordered them to be put on shore, hoping they would in gratitude give a good account of the

Russians to their countrymen.

In their place, I determined to take four seamen from the Japanese vessel who might be useful in attending Takataya-Kahei, and left him the choice of individuals. But he earnestly disliked this arrangement and insisted that none of the seamen be removed from his ship. As they were extremely stupid, and Kahei feared they would die of grief owing to the dread caused by mingling with the Russians. The earnestness of his solicitations on this subject led me in some measure to doubt that our comrades were really alive in Matsumae, and I repeated in a decisive manner my determination to take four seamen on board the *Diana*. Then, he begged me to accompany him to his ship.

When we went on board, he assembled the whole of his crew in the cabin; having seated himself on a fine mat, he requested that I take my place next to him. The sailors all knelt down before us, and he delivered a long speech stating that some of them would be accompanying us to Russia.

A very affecting scene was then occurred. A number of the seamen approached him with their heads bent down, and with great eagerness whispered something to him. Their countenances were turned in tears. Even Takataya-Kahei who, up to this moment maintained calmness and resolution, seemed now deeply distressed and began to weep.

I hesitated to carry my resolution into effect for some time with the consideration that I would hereafter have the opportunity of questioning each individual separately. And probably, I could thereby ascertain whether or not our comrades were really alive in Matsumae. I had in other respects no reason to repent of this arrangement for the Natschalnik who was a man of rank, accustomed to live in a style of Asiatic luxury, and who might experience serious inconveniences on our vessel without his Japanese attendants. Two of the seamen could be always near Kahei by turns. As he knew the reasons which obliged me to take him to Russia, and the message which Leonsaimon received from the commandant of Kunashiri Island, I asked him to write a brief explanation to the latter of all that had happened.

He immediately drew up a letter, after asking the name of our ship, at what time we set sail for Kunashiri, who Leonsaimon was, and so on. Takataya-Kahei, and the sailors he selected were not prisoners, but soon they behaved as if our ship were their own. And we employed every means to convince them that we considered the Japanese not as a hostile, but as a friendly nation. Our good relations were only accidently interrupted.

On the same day, a Japanese lady from the

captured vessel visited our ship at my invitation. She had been a companion of Takataya-Kahei on his voyage from Hakodate, his place of residence, to Etorofu. She was extremely interested in our ship and the strange but polite enemy, and she scrutinized our friendly intercourse with her countrymen. To us, the Japanese lady was not a slight curiosity. She appeared very timid and embarrassed when she came on board. I requested Takataya-Kahei to bring her into my cabin; as she showed some hesitation to advance, I took her by the other hand. On reaching the cabin door she wished to take off her straw shoes; by signs, I explained to her that this was unnecessary as there were no mats and no carpets in my cabin.

This singular mark of politeness might have created a new atmosphere among us. On entering the cabin, she placed both hands on her head, with the palms outward, and saluted us by bending her body very low. I offered a chair, and Kahei asked her to sit. Fortunately there was another young and handsome woman for this unexpected visitor. The wife of our surgeon's mate was on our vessel. The Japanese lady seemed highly pleased at being introduced to her.

Quickly they became acquainted, and she behaved with all the interest of a woman of fashion. She examined the ornaments with great curiosity, and expressed her admiration by an agreeable smile. But what most attracted her attention seemed to be the fair complexion of our countrywoman. She passed her hands over her face as if she suspected it had been painted. And with a smile, she exclaimed, *"Yoee! Yoee!"* which meant "Good!" She was somewhat interested in her new ornaments, and I held a mirror before her so that she might see how they became her. The Russian lady placed herself immediately behind her to show her the difference between their complexions. She immediately pushed the mirror aside, and said with good humor, *"Waree! Waree!"* which meant "Not good!" She might have been called handsome. Her face was oval, her features regular, and her little mouth when it was open disclosed a set of shining black lacquered teeth. Her black eyebrows, which had the appearance of being penciled, over-arched a pair of sparkling dark eyes, which were by no means deeply seated. Her hair was black and rolled up in the form of a turban without any ornament except a few small tortoise-shell combs.

She was of intermediate size, and elegantly formed. Her dress consisted of six layered silk garments, similar to our night gowns, each fastened around the lower waist by separate band, and drawn close together from the girdle downward. They were all different colors, and the uppermost one was black. Her articulation was slow, and her voice was soft. Her countenance was expressive and interesting, and altogether calculated to make a very agreeable impression. She could not have been older than eighteen. We entertained her with fine green tea and sweetmeats which she ate and drank moderately.

On her departure I made some presents, with which she appeared to be very much pleased. I hinted to our countrywoman that she should embrace her. When the Japanese observed what was intended, she ran into her arms, and kissed her with a smile. Finally, she was landed on Kunashiri by the same baidare which carried Takataya-Kahei's letter.

I was now confident that the governor of the island would send us a written communication, if not to me at least to Takataya-Kahei, and also hoped that he would order Leonsaimon to return and serve as our interpreter. But instead of receiving any answers, we had four guns fired at our boats a few days later, when they went on shore for water. We therefore concluded that the governor had received orders from his government to hold no communications with us. I despised this inefficient firing and wishing to examine all my prisoners thoroughly, I determined not to engage in any rash action which might defeat our main purpose.

As the weather continued to be fair, I gave the order to weigh the anchor. Then Takataya-Kahei requested permission for the sailors of his vessel to tour the *Diana*. Japanese sailors were admitted onboard the ship by turns, and were very eager to be acquainted with the use of everything that was new to them. They particularly admired the mechanism of our rigging, the bold climbing of our sailors up the futtock shrouds, and the still more daring manner in which they ran from the tops out upon the yards, or ascended to the mast-head. I gave orders to take them into my cabin where they made the same demonstrations of respect as if I had been present.

Russian vodka was served to them in silver cups, the influence of which soon made them more lively and unreserved in manner. They contrived to make themselves understood by our sailors, and seemed much pleased with our clothes, shining buttons and colored cravats, which they convinced the seamen to exchange for some Japanese trifles.

Takataya-Kahei observed some empty casks on the deck, and proposed they should be sent to his ship for filling. His seamen immediately carried off all our empty casks, and brought them back filled with excellent fresh water. The good-natured Japanese then left our ship, and sang as they returned to their vessel. We were much gratified at finding ourselves so friendly with these men whom we had looked up as our enemies a short time ago.

In the evening we weighed the anchor, and immediately all the batteries opened the fire. It was probably suspected that we intended to approach the fortress with hostile intention. But we were such a great distance from the batteries that the manner in which the Japanese threw away their shot was truly laughable. Our guest likewise laughed and sad,

"Kunashiri is a bad place for Russians; Nangasaki is better."

On the following day, adverse winds obliged us to cast anchor in the bay, at a distance of more than seven leagues from the village. We anxiously watched with our telescopes for the return of the baidare which was sent to shore. Kahei, however, assured us that the baidare would not be allowed to return while our vessel remained in sight of the island.

On September 11 we began a voyage, directing our course toward Kamchatka. During our passage we encountered several violent storms. Storms during this season of the year were dreadful in all the seas under these latitudes. On the day of our departure, we were in peril for twelve hours and only God could have released us. Toward noon a smart gale arose, which soon exploded into a violent hurricane. The low islands between Kunashiri and Shikotan lay to leeward.

The *Diana* worked well to windward, but it

appeared there was a current, which, in spite of all our efforts, carried us toward these islands. The current was running so fast that we could not hope to bring up. We were driven from the open sea into the strait between Kunashiri and Shikotan, and we were in the greatest danger of being wrecked. Every time the lead was cast we observed that we were drawing nearer to the dreadful islands. At half-past three in the morning we found that the water depth had decreased from eighteen to thirteen fathoms, and the ship was pushed by the current facing broadside toward the island. In this desperate situation we resorted to the last means that might save us.

We cast out an anchor, but it would not hold on the sand and gravel bottom. The lead showed the water depth had further decreased by two fathoms. Another anchor was cast, and it started dragging. It caused the ship to lie almost on her beam ends with the waves breaking over her. At last, having all our yards and top-masts down, the ship fortunately regained the right position and the anchor worked. Thus we escaped inevitable destruction and survived.

As Takataya-Kahei occupied the same cabin with me, I had every opportunity to communicate with him. Yet, I strove in vain for a long time to collect information regarding Golownin from him. He listened very attentively to the description I gave him about Golownin's rank and name, but constantly repeated, *"I know nothing about him."*

Now I became aware that our Russian family names must have a singular sound in the ear of the Japanese. I endeavored to pronounce the name, *"Golownin"* in all the different ways I could think of, and at length, to my indescribable joy, Kahei exclaimed, *"Choworin!"* *"I have heard of him! He is, likewise, in Matsumae"* The Japanese supposed him to be a Russian daimyo. *(governor of territorial clan)* Kahei then proceeded to inform me what he had heard regarding Captain Golownin from a person who had seen him.

He was tall, of stately deportment and more reserved in his manners than Mr. Moor, and not fond of smoking tobacco, though the Japanese gave him the best that could be procured. Mr. Moor on the contrary loved to smoke a pipe, and understood the Japanese language tolerably well. These minute descriptions banished all our doubts, and we thanked for God having sent us a guest capable of communicating such pleasing intelligence.

I was filled with overwhelming joy that I had doubted the truth of the answer brought by Leonsaimon, and had not proceeded to hostilities as I intended at first. I learned from our prisoner that he sailed every year to Etorofu with goods of various kinds, and returned with fish. I was much astonished at him not knowing Leonsaimon.

I wondered if I did not pronounce the name right, and showed Kahei my memorandum in which Leonsaimon had written his own name and that of his native town Matsumae. Kahei read the signature, and declared that no merchant of that name had ever lived at Etorofu; he added that he knew everyone on the island, and he even told me their names. I now repeated all the names which Leonsaimon attributed to himself: Nagachema, Tomogero and <u>Gorogee</u>. On hearing the last name, he laughed and exclaimed with astonishment. *"What, Gorogee! I know him!"*

And so he represented himself in Russia as an <u>Oyakata.</u> *(chief of the Kuriles)* I answered, *"Yes"* and he stated that he was a wealthy man. Kahei replied, *"Gorogee never possessed a single baidare. He was a banin."* *(fishery watcher)* He was also in charge of the correspondence as he had a good command of writing. He was not a native of Matsumae, but of the Principality of <u>Nambu</u> and was married to the daughter of a hairy Kurile. Kahei uttered these last words with a contemptuous expression, and drew his hand across his throat, as if to signify that Leonsaimon's head would be chopped off if his false declaration on his position and marriage were known to the Japanese government.

This unexpected discovery induced me to believe that the Japanese I sent to the governor of the island, might yield to wicked instigations, or might act treacherously in order to gratify a base revenge.

Besides, it appeared that I was wrong in attributing the escape of the Japanese, who had left Leonsaimon near the fortress, to the fear of returning to us. For I have learned from Takataya-Kahei that Japanese who lived more than one year in a foreign country are prohibited on their return home from repairing under any pretense to their own families. They are sent to Edo for investigation, where they are generally detained for the rest of their lives, without hope of ever seeing their friends again. Our Japanese lived about one year in Kamchatka, and that circumstance accounted for their non-appearance.

As we were leaving the stormy coasts of Japan, we soon found ourselves among the Kurile Islands off <u>La Bussole Strait</u> named by the celebrated La Perouse. The weather was sufficiently clear to make astronomical observations. We purposely sailed through this wide strait into the sea of Okhotsk, and observed the western coasts of some island, situated toward the north. We then passed into the eastern ocean, through an unexplored strait, between the islands of <u>Raikoke</u> and <u>Matua</u>.

As this strait had, as yet, received no

designation on any chart, I gave it the name of Golownin, as a mark of respect to our unfortunate captain who had contributed so much to our voyages in these seas.

On September 22 we discovered the top of the extinguished volcano of Kamchatka, which was covered with snow. The valleys, however, were beautifully verdant, and the temperature of the atmosphere was mild. Kahei observed that in the course of his voyage to Etorofu and Urup in the same season of the year, he had seen more snow on the coasts of these islands, and had experienced a degree of cold far more severe. We approached the Bay of Awatscha with favorable winds, and hoped to enter the harbor of Petrepaulowski on the following day. But the wind changed, and we were twice driven out to sea.   For the third time, we were in great danger of shipwreck during a dark night while we were working up with great difficulty.

We entered the harbor on October 3, where we found three ships, one freighter from Okhotsk and the other two bearing the American flag and belonging to Mr. Dobell, a citizen of the United States. One had a cargo from Kanton and the other had a cargo from Manila. Mr. Dobell himself commanded one of vessels, and formed an excellent plan for establishing commercial relations between China and

Kamchatka, or other countries possessing valuable products in the area.

My first objective was to send our good Japanese on shore. He appeared extremely disconsolate, but I attributed this to the protracted hardships which he had endured on the voyage. His distress however arose from a very different cause. Our friends came from the shore to congratulate us on our safe arrival, and Kahei now began to lament his fate. Judging from the laws of his own country he supposed he would be kept as a prisoner like our comrades in Japan. But he was much astonished, for he was allowed to reside not merely in the same house but in the same apartment as me.

On October 12 we went ashore together, after giving a party on the ship to celebrate our triple escape from shipwreck. Thus, we terminated our first voyage to Japan and the result was the satisfaction of knowing that our comrades were still in existence, which proved an ample reward for all the hardships we went through.

— The Second Voyage —

In the past twenty years, Takataya-Kahei had sailed to most of the harbors around the country.

He had managed to acquire a great knowledge of navigation, and he carried out considerable trade business. It was obvious that he was a prominent person in his government. His sophisticated manners were evidence enough that he belonged to a superior class of society.

I reluctantly happened to be the author of his misfortune, and the only consolation I found was that Kahei did not show any despondency. On the contrary, he cheered himself with the patriotic idea that he would be able to prove that our government entertained no hostile designs toward Japan. Kahei pledged Golownin's existence and the immediate liberation of our comrades if a diplomatic delegate were sent to Nagasaki.

While we enjoyed a man of society so well informed, and so entirely devoted to our interest, I was mortified that the Japanese interpreter from Irkutzk was not with us, and could not possibly visit Kamchatka until the following year.

However, our mutual anxiety to become intelligible to each other induced Kahei to learn Russian in the course of the winter, and we were soon able to exchange words even on abstract subjects. I told him of all the imprudent transactions that had excited the displeasure of the Japanese. When our delegate to Nagasaki turned out abortive, I was able to discuss that with him as well. He said that when the arrival of the Russian ships was known at Nagasaki, all the Japanese earnestly wished for the adoption of a commercial treaty with Russia.

When certain event a "cruel aggression" was Kahei's expression led to the dismissal of delegates, all of Japan was displeased with their government. While communicating information regarding his country, and expressing his wish to see trade opened between Russia and Japan, Kahei often said, *"I perceive in my misfortune, God has chosen me as his instrument. I had no important reason for putting into the Bay of Kunashiri; it happened accidentally. I had not been there for five years, and I came in time to prevent your hostile attack, where I saved some dozens of Russians and perhaps hundreds of Japanese. This idea animates me, and I hope, despite my poor health conditions, to overcome the severe climate of Kamchatka."*

The attention and sympathy which all the Russians manifested toward Kahei deeply affected the heart of this worthy man. He meditated day and night on drawing up a report to his government in which he intended to give a very different impression of the Russians from any report previously presented by the Japanese. Far superior in education and understanding to any of the Japanese who had formerly been among us, he clearly perceived that the good of his country, upon which he never reflected without emotion, required an amicable adjustment of the differences between Russia and Japan; he perceived also that this adjustment was solely up to Japan. He was convinced that his country would be the principal of sufferer if these differences continued.

He therefore strove to represent the singular conduct of the Japanese as well as their laws and customs, which were calculated to excite prejudice in the minds of foreigners. He observed that they never entertained the conduct of carrying on a useless contest with a powerful neighboring empire, though the transgression of some of our countrymen had obliged them to take up arms in their own defense, and had raised an idea in their minds that Russia entertained hostile conduct against Japan. If Japan had a dialogue or received a memorandum or, like other powers, maintained relationships with her neighbors, Japan would not force countermeasures.

Trade with other countries was, however, prohibited by their law. And it was consequently impossible for them to ascertain whether or not those atrocities were committed by order of our government. Preparations for countermeasure were then made throughout Japan, but the object of the Japanese was merely to obtain an explanation from the Russian government. Kahei said, *"I am confident that a message from the governor of Irkutzk, declaring that Chwostoff's aggression was totally unauthorized, would be sufficient to obtain the liberation of your comrades."*

These were not merely empty words, nor uttered by Kahei with the intent of accelerating his liberation. We had subsequently the full evidence of their truth. Kahei actually became the instrument whereby the differences between the two powers were adjusted and the deliverance of our comrades was accomplished. As some points if not very important, were yet opposed to the laws of the Japanese empire, he would work to firmly establish the difference for the future.

I briefly reported to the commandant of Okhotsk all that had taken place, and requested that he furnishes me with an official letter from the governor of Irkutzk to the bugyo of Matsumae. I added that I was ready to proceed to Okhotsk myself to obtain this letter, and that Takataya-Kahei had undertaken to deliver it personally to the bugyo. We were to land Kahei at Kunashiri. He proposed to transmit decisive answers and information regarding our comrades. Such was the plan we laid down for our future expedition.

Kahei continued tranquil and in good health

until the middle of winter, when the death of his two attendants greatly affected him. He then became melancholy and peevish. He constantly complained of indisposition and asserted that he had scurvy in his feet, which, he told the surgeon, would certainly cause his death.

Our surgeon was however well aware, that his real disorder was nostalgia, or an anxiety for home. He feared that he would be detained in Okhotsk, where I intended to take him, and finally disclosed this apprehension to me, as the whole success of our plan depended on his safe return to his country.   I immediately determined to tell him about that we planned to depart for Japan without waiting for an answer from Irkutzk. When I informed him of this resolution, he called his two remaining seamen and communicated the joyful intelligence to them. He then requested that I allow him a few moments of privacy with his two attendants.   I withdrew into the next room, believing they wished to pray without any witnesses present, but he soon came to me dressed in state dress with his sword by his side and his two attendants behind him. Then, he made a speech to strongly express his gratitude. I was indeed surprised and moved, and again vowed to him the fulfillment of my promise.

In April, when we began to prepare for our voyage, I received orders from the governor of Irkutzk, to put our plan into execution as a Naval Commander at Kamchatka. In case I should sail again for the Japanese coast, he suggested that I leave Lieutenant Rudakoff in command of the station as my substitute. In consequence of these orders, I took Lieutenant Filatoff, who commanded the *Sotik* brig on board of the *Diana* to fill the place of Lieutenant Rudakoff. The *Sotik*, which was separated from the *Diana* in the storm off Kunashiri in the previous autumn, was afterward wrecked on the coast of Kamchatka. But the crews and part of the stores were saved by Lieutenant Filatoff.

On May 6 we cut through the ice and maneuvered the *Diana* into the Bay of Awatscha and we departed on the May 23. After a favorable voyage of twenty days, we cast anchor in the Bay of Deceit, at about the same distance from the Japanese fortifications as the previous year. In pursuance of Takataya-Kahei's advice, his two sailors desired to prepare for proceeding on shore. The buildings were as formerly concealed by striped cotton cloth. No guns were fired, but not a single creature was found on the whole coast. Before their departure, the two Japanese sailors came into the cabin to thank me, and to receive the message which their Natschalnik wished to send to the Natschalnik of the island.

I took this opportunity to ask Takataya-Kahei whether he had commissioned his sailors to bring back circumstantial information regarding my comrades, and whether he pledged himself for their return. He answered in the negative. I was startled at his refusal. He said, *"You are surprised, because you do not know our laws."* I replied, *"Indeed, I do not know them all. But since it is so,"* turning to the Japanese sailors, "*Tell the governor of Kunashiri from me, if he prevents you from returning, and permits me to receive no information, I will carry your Natschalnik back to Okhotsk, where some war ships with armed men on board will be ready for this year, and I will demand the liberation of the Russian prisoners. I will only wait three days for the answer."*

At these words Takataya-Kahei's countenance changed, but he said with much calmness, *"Commander of the Imperial Ship!"* He always addressed me thus on important occasions.

"You counseled rashly. Your orders to the governor of Kunashiri seem to contain much, but according to our laws, they should contain little. It is in vain to threaten to take me to Okhotsk. My men may be detained on shore but neither two nor two thousand sailors can bring answer for me. As I told you previously, you don't have such power to take me to

Okhotsk. But, tell me if you really intend to send my sailors on shore under only these conditions"

I said, *"Yes, as a commander of the warship, under these circumstances, I cannot act otherwise."*

He replied, *"Well, allow me to give my last words to my sailors and most urgent instructions regarding what they must convey from me to the governor of Kunashiri. For now I will not send a promised letter, not even any other written documents."*

After this conversation, he sat according to the Japanese custom with his legs under him. He then stood up and addressed me very earnestly with the following words: *"You know enough of Japanese to understand all that I may say in plain and simple words to my sailors. I would not wish that you have any grounds to suspect me."*

He sat down again when his sailors approached him on their knees hanging down their heads, they listened with utmost attention to his words. He then reminded them of the day they were carried on board the *Diana*, and of the manner they were treated on board the ship and in Kamchatka, and of the death of two attendants and the Kurile. All possible attentions had been bestowed on them by the Russian physician, and finally the ship had hastily returned to Japan for Kahei's health.

Of all these facts he reminded them

faithfully, and he concluded with the warmest commendations of me, and earnest expressions of gratitude for the care I had extended to him at sea and on land. He came to a deep silence and prayed. Then, he delivered to the sailor he most esteemed his picture, to be handed to his wife, and his large sword, which he called his paternal sword, to be handed to his only son and heir.   After this solemn ceremony was over, he stood up, and with frankness and a very cheerful expression, he asked me for some <u>vodka</u> as a farewell treat for his sailors.

He drank with them and accompanied them on deck without giving them any further instructions. Then, we saw them ashore, and they proceeded toward the fortress without interruption. All that had passed with the significant words between Kahei and the sailors who were separated from him, together with the ominous words, *"It will not be in your power to take me to Okhotsk,"* gave me much anxiety. The return of the sailors appeared very uncertain to me. I could retain their sick master as a hostage, but I could not stop his rash speech. Whether or not I should put him on shore was a matter of difficult decision.

Yet, when all circumstances were considered, releasing Kahei appeared likely to prove the more beneficial to our imprisoned comrades. In case he did not return, I am determined to advance immediately to the fortress. I knew enough Japanese to make myself understood, and I thought if our comrades were still alive, such an advance could not render their fate worse.

   If they were dead, the whole affair together with all my anxieties would be swiftly brought to a decision. I conveyed my ideas to my senior officers, as it was necessary to give him early information, in consequence of the execution of remaining duties to complete. As he concurred with me, I told Kahei, that he might go on shore once he promised, and I trusted his return. If he did not return it would cost me my life. He answered, *"I understand you cannot return to Okhotsk without a written testimonial on the fate of your comrades, and for my part no slightest stain on my honor will be at the expense of my life. I wish to thank you for the confidence placed in me. I had resolved not to go on shore on the same day with my sailors. According to our custom, that is not the way I should take. Now, if you have no objections, I will go ashore early tomorrow."*

   I answered, *"I will take you by myself."* Then, he exclaimed, *"For three hundred days, you never spoke unkind words to me, even though I frequently yielded without any cause to my fiery temperament. Then, we were friends again!*

I will now tell you what I meant by sending away my portrait and my paternal sword. But I must first confess, with that candor which I have invariably observed toward you for the period of three hundred days, that I was much offended by your message to the governor of Kunashiri. The threat to send ships of war here during the present year did not concern me, but on hearing your threat to take me to Okhotsk, I believed that you did regard me as an impostor as great as Gorogee (Leonsaimon) — I could, indeed, scarcely persuade myself that your lips could utter such an injury to my honor."

"But, on this important occasion, anger over came your reason, and for a moment your idea drove me to become a criminal and commit suicide. That a man of my rank should remain as a prisoner in a foreign country is repugnant to our national honor. Yet even though you might reduce me to that condition, I would be accompanied to Kamchatka. My government was informed of that circumstance, for I sent a message to Kunashiri explaining your reason for visiting my ship. The sailors alone were compelled to accompany you against their inclination."

"You were the strongest party, but though my body was in your power, my soul was not at your disposal. I will now disclose the secret in my heart. I had determined to commit suicide in case your

*purpose remained unchanged. I therefore cut the
central tuft of hair from the head."* He showed me
the part where the hair was removed and laid it in the
box with the portrait.

*"According to our Japanese customs, this
signifies the person who sends his hair in this manner
to his friends has died an honorable death. That is to
say, honorable death is the same as <u>Hara-Kiri.</u> Then,
his hair is buried with all the respects of the
interment of his body. You called me friend, and
therefore I conceal nothing from you. Irritation was so
great that I would have killed both you and the senior
officer for the mere satisfaction of disclosing what
happened to your subordinate crews."*

What a strange sense of honor according to
European ideas! But the Japanese consider such
conduct to be the most honorable. The memory of the
hero is preserved with respect, and the honor of the
deed passes to his posterity. If, on the contrary, he
should fail to act in this manner, his children are
banished from the place of their birth.

I lived with a man with these terrible ideas
in the same cabin, and slept tranquilly near him, in
the confidence of perfect security. While shocked by
the discovery of the danger from which I had escaped,
I could not help asking him why he was so limited in
his vengeance, as it was in his power to destroy us all

by setting fire to the magazine.

He said, *"No, what bravery would there be! A coward alone would satiate his revenge in such a manner. Do you imagine that I kill you while in sleep, a person I honor as valiant Natschalink ? No! I will work more fairly."*

Extraordinary man! After this I esteemed him more highly than before. The next day I got onboard with my reconciled friend and sailed for the shore. As we approached, we saw two Japanese coming out of the fortress, and to our great joy we recognized them to be Takataya-Kahei's sailors. We landed and waited for them beside the stream opposite to where our ship lay.

They informed us that the governor of Kunashiri had received them kindly, and had granted my request regarding the supply of water on the condition that I should not allow my men to land on that side of the river near the fortress. They added that three officers were already in Kunashiri, and mentioned their names. Takataya-Kahei recognized two of them as his intimate friends.

The sailors knew nothing further than this, except that the governor had expressed a desire to speak with their master as soon as possible. He had noticed some trifles which I had given them as gifts and would not permit them to retain anything. They accordingly brought back every article, even pins and needles, all untouched in a parcel. I thought this was an indication of no friendly disposition, but Kahei erased my apprehensions by informing me that the Japanese laws prohibited receiving these gifts from his comrades.

One of the sailors delivered me a box full of papers that was sent by the governor of Matsumae. I eagerly proceeded to open it, in the expectation of finding letters from my captured comrades, but Takataya-Kahei prevented me. He said, *"Repress your curiosity, as the box may contain important papers from the governor."*

He then took it from me. He observed his usual demonstrations of respect, and raised the box three times above his head.   And he said,   *"All is favorable to us!   I say to us, for I now feel half a Russian. Everything will be fine if you permit me to carry the box back to the governor. Tomorrow morning I will not fail to bring it back to you. Such are the forms which the customs of our country render necessary."*

I hesitated for a few moments but suddenly recollected myself, and without manifesting the slightest distrust, I declared that I would follow his advice. I split one of my handkerchiefs through the middle, and handed him one of the pieces, saying,

"I will regard as a friend whoever brings back this half of my handkerchief within two or three days at the latest." He replied in a firm tone of voice that death alone should prevent him from fulfilling that duty. The next morning he would return on board the ship; in the meantime he wished me to allow his seamen to accompany him. I readily accepted this and went on board. I made the ship to be kept ready for action during the night.

On the following day our sentinels informed me that they observed two men apart from the garrison, and one of them carried something while his hand was constantly waving something white. This proved to be Kahei. I immediately sent out the boat, and soon he arrived, accompanied by one of his sailors. To our great joy, he told us that according to the letter from Matsumae, all of our comrades were well, except the navigator, who was so dangerously ill that he had tasted nothing for ten days, and moreover refused to follow the prescription of the Japanese physicians.

The latest account, however, stated that this man had recovered in some measure. Kahei then delivered to me in the cabin, the official paper which had been in the box. It was a letter from the Matsu-mae Bugyo to the commandant of Kunashiri, written in the Japanese language with a Russian translation. I gave Kahei a note acknowledging the receipt of this paper, to be taken back with him to Kunashiri, and by his advice I also declared my readiness to sail straight to Hakodate, on the condition that two Japanese should be allowed to accompany me so that I might be enabled to commence regular communications.

Kahei undertook to explain to the commandant the contents of this letter, and in the evening we put him ashore. Kahei returned next day, despite the rainy state of the weather, and told us that although the governor considered my proposal was extremely reasonable, he was not authorized to act on his own opinion in this case. Therefore he sent a courier to Matsumae with my last letter and the one which I wrote when I first arrived at Kunashiri.

Kahei said, *"There are Russian interpreters in Matsumae,"* He assured me that the letter would return in twenty days. Taking all these favorable circumstances into consideration, I resolved to wait for the answer from the Matsumae Bugyo.

In the meantime, I wished to conduct a correct survey of the Bay of Deceit. For this purpose, I asked the commandant of Kunashiri to permit the boat to sail in various directions. However, he sent me a very polite answer stating that his instructions obliged him to decline granting the permission. Therefore, we could only land at the rivulet already mentioned, and on the condition stated before. This reply was couched with very civil terms, and afforded us at least some consolation.

Meanwhile, Kahei on every third day brought us information of all that took place. His sailors frequently brought us presents of fish in his name, which I distributed among the crew in equal portions. He gave strict orders that they should receive no payment in return for these presents, and always expressed his regret that the poor fish catch prevented him from being more liberal in his gifts. Indeed we did not receive more than seventeen fish during the whole time.

Whenever Kahei came on board our ship, the day was always observed as a holyday. His first visit took place on July 14. In the course of our confidential conversation, I observed that I had read the letter from Matsumae several times over, and that I was astonished to find that it contained no mention of a very important issue, the reason why Kahei became our prisoner. At this remark, he himself seemed surprised at first, and frequently made use of the emphatic Japanese exclamation, *"Fushigi !"* But after a little reflection, he said, *"No, it is easily accounted for. According to our laws, you were justified in proceeding with hostilities after being informed that your comrades were dead. Even if you put me and all my crew to the death, our government*

72

would still take no notice of the event under the present circumstances. I confirmed that Gorogee did not deceive you, but the answer that he delivered to you was that of the commandant who was greatly irritated by the attack of Chwostoff! He burned with the desire to measure his strength against yours, and anxiously awaited the moment when you should attack the fortress. The whole garrison, consisting of about three hundred Japanese, swore to perish with sword in hand. Therefore, according to the customs of war, they prepared for their funerals while living; every man cut the tuft of hair from the crown of his head, and these were all deposited in one box, each wrapped in a separate piece of paper inscribed with the individual name.

   On your first hostile movement, this box was to be forwarded to Matsumae. As I know your spirit, I am well aware that horrible carnage would have ensued. The superiority of your artillery might ensure you the victory, but it would last for only a short duration. For the Japanese learned from the aggression of Chwostoff's crew that your countrymen are passionately fond of strong liquors, and therefore they were prepared to poison all the spirits. Then, few of your people could escape death."

   He also stated, that the commandant regretted he could not supply us with fresh provisions, but even though the fishing season had not yet commenced, boats were sent out for the purpose of catching fish. Kahei himself promised to bring us some on the first draught, though we requested him not give himself so much trouble. He replied, *"It cannot be too much. The first fruits of our labor should be always presented to our friend."* We landed him again at the rivulet, and he had to walk at least two wersts to the fortress. Bad weather prevented him from visiting us next day.

On July 16, however, he came so early that our sentinels did not perceive him until he had reached the rivulet and was waiting for our boat. I was vexed at this accident, and I made an apology on his arrival, observing that we could not expect him to sacrifice his rest in such a way.

He frankly acknowledged that he felt offended at the delay. He said, *"From the moment I left the garrison, I continued to wave the white handkerchief and if the boat had delayed a few moments longer to meet me, I would certainly have left the place."* I thought it proper to reprimand the sentinels in the presence of this punctilious old man.

He added, *"You seem surprised with my early return. The governor endeavored to dissuade me from coming, but it is impossible to break one's word. Yesterday I spent a miserable day. I waited for the return of the fisherman until it was too late to come to you. I could not enjoy a moment's sleep in consequence of not fulfilling my promise. As soon as morning light told us to get up, we took a cup of tea and hastened with all the fish which we caught yesterday. As you see, there are only fourteen in number but today I shall enjoy the satisfaction of partaking of the first fresh fish with your company, for I ate none on the shore."*

What cordiality! I attempted to express my appreciation, but merely said, *"You are my friend, and friends understand each other."*

Our dinner was served early as Kahei repeatedly mentioned his starvation and his appetite. The fish, cooked with common Japanese grits, was served. Kahei satisfied his appetite with an uncommonly hearty dinner; I thought I had never tasted fish of finer flavor, for the meal was seasoned by friendship. After the dinner we toasted to the health of the worthy Kahei, and by the late evening we put him on shore.

On July 18 he entered again into a friendly conversation; in the course of it he complained of the tedious life he lived on shore, and of the person he lived with. He was the agent of the merchants who received designation of business on the island. Kahei differed with this man. Therefore, with the governor's consent, he procured thirty Kuriles and built a wooden house, where he said he could live quietly with his two sailors. He spoke with great contempt of this agent and the company of the merchant; in the end, he described them with a pithy Japanese proverb: *"Penniless but proud."*

On July 20 I was informed that the sentinels had again observed our <u>Taisho</u>.   Kahei was known by this title among the sailors. In Japanese, *"Taisho"* signifies *"commander."*   He used the word when he first addressed me, and I returned the compliment since the seamen constantly called him Taisho.   I conjectured that the languor he experienced on shore induced him to pay us this visit before the stipulated term. I therefore showed no suspicion when he came on board, but conducted him straight to the cabin. He sat down beside me, and without any remarkable expression of countenance, he said, *"This unsealed letter, written as it appears in Russian, arrived at this moment from Matsumae."*

Lieutenant Filatoff, who was present cast a glance at the superscription and exclaimed in ecstasy, *"It is the handwriting of our Wassili Michailovitch!"*

My joy knew no bounds; I snatched the letter from the hand of my friend Kahei, and recognized Golownin's writing, and imagined from the size of the paper that it contained an account of the events of his captivity but when I unfolded the letter I found merely the following lines:

We are all, both officers and seamen, and the Kurile Alexei, alive and reside in Matsumae.	
	WASSILI GOLOWNIN,
May 10, 1813	FEODOR MOOR

I took these gratifying lines, which removed every doubt about the existence of our comrades, and read them on deck to the crew. Many of the men, who knew the writing of their adored captain, perused the letter themselves, and greeted Takataya-Kahei with cheers. Grog was served to the whole ship company, to toast the health of their officers and friends. For they had all been willing to sacrifice their lives on this coast in the previous year.

On this occasion the Taisho informed me of a happy event. He had received a letter from his son in Hakodate, which the governor had conveyed to him in the following singular manner.   According to the Japanese laws, a person immediately returned from a foreign country is not allowed to correspond or meet with others. The governor therefore ordered Kahei to be called, as if merely for the purpose of giving him Captain Golownin's letter to take on board the *Diana*. He didn't say a word; however, while walking up and down the room, he threw a letter from Kahei's son towards him, as if it were a useless piece of paper taken out of his pocket with the other letter. Then, he turned his back to give Kahei time to pick up. Kahei understood perfectly well what he meant, and without any embarrassment, he picked up the letter and placed it in his pocket.

His son had written to inform him that his commercial business had been in the most advantageous circumstances. The number of ships had increased, and a couple of ships were just launched. Kahei's mother and his beloved wife were both in good health, but in her grief while Kahei was in Kamchatka, his wife had begun a pilgrimage throughout Japan. She was visiting the most celebrated shrines and had not yet returned.

A rich man, Kahei's bosom friend, had learned Kahei's fate, and he had distributed his property among the poor, and moved his residence into the mountains where he lived as a hermit. What an example! Among Europeans, the Japanese were regarded as crafty, base, vengeful, and incapable of the delicate feelings of friendship!

There are indeed in Japan, MEN who deserve that name in the highest sense of the word, and a national virtue which would not be unworthy of our imitation!

I said to Kahei, *"How rich you are in having such a friend! I am indeed rich for I have two such friends."* I exclaimed, *"What two friends ! What a number !"*

     This idea seemed to highly please him. He was further informed that, for several days, his friends had been preparing festivities at different temples in order to be ready to celebrate his return. He was a well-regarded person throughout Japan, and people believed that God would bless him while in Russia and ensure his safe return to his home country. That happy result would spread brightness through-out Japan.

     His son embraced this belief with so much confidence that he prepared this letter in due time to be sent to Kunashiri for the consolation of his father on his return. His son had a perfect conviction that this would take place soon. It was one of the most joyful moments of my life! When Takataya-Kahei left us, he intimated a wish that the sailors might again salute him with cheers. The whole ship's company obliged with a most hearty *"Hurrah!"*

     On July 26 he came on board with the information that the letter had arrived from Matsumae, and that the first counselor of Matsumae Bugyo, who was to communicate the answer to my letter, had embarked on board a Japanese government ship. The Kurile, Alexei, and one of our Russian prisoners were to accompany this mission.

We all supposed that the Russian must be an officer, but our friend understood that he was one of the sailors.

Considering time of the departure, we expected them to arrive on the same day or the following day. In fact, in a few hours, we saw a large ship with a flag. Takataya-Kahei told us it was a government ship with a red globe on her sails. The sides were covered with red stripes and the gangways were decorated with striped cloth. Three flags with variegated colors waved on the stern. There were four long pikes that indicated the rank of the person on board fixed on the same part of the ship. The pikes had floating streamers, each black at the extremity.

On the approach of the vessel, baidares bearing flags left the shore and proceeded closer to meet her. Each supplied a particular boat, bound for towing. Together they towed the ship toward the fortress. It was already dark, and we could not perceive what preparations were made on the shore for the reception of the deputy bugyo but Kahei promised to return the next day with information of all that occurred.

Faithful to his appointment, we saw him in the morning coming down to the shore in company with another man. Kahei was instantly recognized by the white handkerchief which he always waved at the end of his sword, and with respect to the other we did not remain long in uncertainty, for as they advanced, our worthy little friend occasionally vanished from our view in consequence of falling behind his more bulky companion. We all exclaimed, *"That is one of our Russians."*

It is impossible for me to describe the moving scene which followed, when our sailors beheld their comrade returned from captivity. Some of the crew were filling their watercasks at the rivulet. When the prisoner saw Russians on the other side of the stream, and probably recognized among them some of his old messmates, he made one step onto its bank, leaving Kahei at least nine steps behind him. Surprise and joy made our sailors forget that they were prohibited from crossing the rivulet. They waded through it, and embraced the welcome visitor in the most affectionate manner.

The officer who commanded the party on shore informed me that at first he did not know the stranger, he was so altered by the sufferings he had experienced. At last, all the men cried out with one voice, *"Simanoff!"* For that was his name. He then threw off his hat, knelt down, and could not utter a word, but the tears filled his eyes and ran down his cheeks. This affecting spectacle was renewed when he came on board the ship. I saluted him first, and asked whether our friends in Matsumae were well.

He replied, *"God be praised, they are alive though not all quite well.   Mr. Chlebnikoff, in particular, is dangerously ill!"*   I repressed my desire to ask further questions, as I observed the great impatience with which the seamen were waiting to embrace him.

I went down to the cabin with Kahei who informed me, that the first officer of the bugyo of Matsumae, named <u>Takahashi-Sampei,</u> had just arrived.   And the bugyo had commissioned him to communicate several circumstances to me. He took out a letter, and read as follows: —

Takahashi-Sampei testifies his respect to the commandant of Kamchatka, and informs him that in consequence of the letter written to Matsumae, my honorable bugyo *(governor)* sent me to Kunashiri, in order to pay respects and to communicate certain preliminary points regarding the liberation of all Russians. Takahashi-Sampei regrets exceedingly that the laws of Japan do not permit him to confer personally with the commandant. He sensibly feels for the hardships which the officers and crew of the Russian ship underwent in their repeated voyages to Kunashiri and laments the hostilities which occurred. With the permission of the bugyo of Matsumae, I have brought one of the Russian prisoners with me. This prisoner will be permitted to go on board the Russian ship every day to converse with his comrades, on the condition that he always returns at night to the fortress. Takahashi-Sampei requests that the commandant of Kamchatka place full confidence in Takataya-Kahei, who was selected for the negotiation, and who may commence to converse freely with the commandant.

The preliminary official points were as follows: —

1) It must be conveyed to the Japanese government a document, signed and sealed by two Russian commanders of districts, certifying, in conformity with the official papers already transmitted, that Chwostoff, without the consent or knowledge of the Russian Government, had unlawfully committed depredations on the islands of the Hairy Kuriles and on Sakhalin.

2) It is known that Chwostoff disturbed the tranquility of the inhabitants of our settlements, and presumed to carry away the millet, and other commodities that belonged to private individuals, and in general whatever he found to Okhotsk.

Among the properties thus removed were our ammunition of war, including armor, bows and arrows, muskets, and some cannons. With respect to the former articles plundered by Chwostoff, the Japanese government is of opinion that they must now, in consequence of the lapse of time, be totally unfit for use; the latter, however, are not liable to spoil by keeping, and ought, therefore, to be restored lest they should hereafter be regarded as booty stolen from the Japanese through aggression. But though they cannot be decayed or injured by use, they may not perhaps be now in Okhotsk. It is true they could be collected together from different places, but such a collection might, on account of the distance of such places, be now difficult. The Japanese government therefore will be satisfied considering the urgency of the present circumstances, if the commandant of Okhotsk certifies that under the strictest investigation, no plundered property brought by Chwostoff from the Kurile Island and Sakhalin are to be found in that place.

It will be remarked by the reader that the Japanese contrived, with much ingenuity and politeness, to make it be clearly understood that it was well known to them through Leonsaimon what had been done with Chwostoff's booty. Only the strict purport of the passage has been given in the translation, but the whole was very delicately expressed in Japanese.

3) Regarding the hostilities in the preceding year, to which the commandant of Kamchatka has alluded in his letter, the Japanese government in consideration of the existing circumstances then, recognizes such conduct on the part of the commander of a Russian imperial ship as justifiable according to their laws, and has therefore passed it over in silence in their official note. But that Takataya-Kahei, the commander of Japanese ship, had been carried to Kamchatka against his inclination is not consistent with the information of the Japanese government, as the letter received at the time from the SendoFunamochi Takataya-Kahei stated that he proceeded according to his own wish to that place, and only four of his sailors were abducted by force.

4) In order that the negotiations may be brought to a peaceful and satisfactory conclusion, Takahashi-Sampei hopes that the Russian war ship will, in the present year, return with the required certificate from Okhotsk to Hakodate, where both the senior official Kujimoto-Hyogoro and I will wait for the commandant of Kamchatka, to receive from him the said certificate. Then, in accordance with the customs of Japanese law, we will personally advise and jointly cooperate with him in effecting the promised liberation of the Russian prisoners. In the

> meantime, we wish for a favorable voyage for the Russian ship and a speedy return to Hakodate.

Thus ended Kahei's commission. Full of impatience to speak to Simanoff, I desired him to be called into a separate cabin. Finding himself alone with me, he drew out a sheet of fine Japanese paper folded up in a singular form through the worn-out stitches of his jacket. The paper was entirely filled with writing. He said, *"This is a letter to you from Wassili Michailovitsch. I have succeeded in concealing it from the notice of the suspicious Japanese. It contains an account of our sufferings, and some good advice regarding the mode in which you are to proceed."* I eagerly took the letter, and it appeared miraculous that it had reached me. I glanced several times over it. Partly through dread that it might contain some unpleasant news, and partly through joy at the unexpected manner in which the letter reached me, I was so agitated that I could not distinguish one word from another. Within the letter I observed two slips of paper which contained some lines, very closely written by Mr. Chlebnikoff.

I recovered myself, and, to my indescribable joy, read that our unhappy friends still cherished some hope of returning to their native country. Captain Golownin's letter was as follows:

Dearest Friend,

      At length the Japanese seemed to be convinced of the truth of our declarations regarding the peaceful intention of Russia, and the unauthorized conduct of Chwostoff but they require a formal attestation from some Natschalnik of our government, to which the imperial seal must be affixed. It is hoped that when they are fully persuaded of the friendly intentions of Russia, they will enter into commercial relations with us, for they seem already aware of the knavery of the Dutch. We informed them of the letter which fell into the hands of the English, in which the Dutch interpreters of Nagasaki boasted of having produced a decided rift between Resanoff and the Japanese. Nevertheless, when you have any intercourse with them. Be extremely cautious, carry on your conferences only in boats, and always keep at the distance of a gunshot from the shore. However, be not offended at the tardiness of their proceedings. We knew them to deliberate for months on an unimportant affair, which in Europe would have been decided in a day or two. In general, I would recommend these four principal requisites to be observed: prudence, patience, civility, and candor.

      On your discretion depends not merely our liberation, but also the interests of our country. May our present misfortune be the means of restoring to Russia those advantages which she lost through the misconduct of one individual!

— but the sailor who is the bearer of this will acquaint you more circumstantially with my opinion on these subjects. It is not convenient to load him with papers, and therefore I do not myself write to the minister.

Where the honor of my sovereign and the interest of my country are concerned, I do not set the value of kopeck on my life; therefore don't take my safety into consideration. Be it now, or ten or twenty years hence, sooner or later, we must all pay the debt of nature. It is immaterial to me whether I die in battle or by the hand of treachery—whether I perish amidst of the waves of the sea, or yield my last breath on a bed of down. Death is always Death, though he may present himself under a variety of forms.

I beg my dearest friend that you will write in my stead to my brother and my friends. Providence may have ordained that I shall see them again or perhaps not. In the latter case, tell them not to be distressed on account of my fate, and that I wish them health and every happiness. I entreat you, in the name of Heaven, to suffer no one to write to me or to send any thing which may occasion me to be tormented by translations and questions but state your own determination in a few lines.

I request that you will give the sailor who is the bearer of this letter five hundred rubles from my effect. Present my sincere respects to our comrades, the officers of the *Diana*, and remember me to all the seamen. With the deepest gratitude, I return you thanks for the many dangers you have encountered for the sake of obtaining our freedom. Adieu, dear friend! And all dear friends, Adieu! This letter is probably the last you will ever receive from me. May you enjoy health, contentment and happiness!

April 10th, 1813.
In the city of Matsumae, in Japanese imprisonment. Your most faithful,

WASSILI GOLOWNIN

In this letter, Captain Golownin warned me against relying too confidently on the apparent sincerity of the Japanese, and hinted that I might obtain, through the bearer, his advice regarding the conduct I should adopt in case affairs took an unfavorable turn. But Simanoff was so overjoyed at the liberty he obtained, and at the opportunity of mixing with his shipmates, that he behaved through-out like one who had lost his wits. Whenever I sought to be made acquainted with instructions, he constantly replied, *"Why do you question me, sir? The letter contains all the information you can stand in need of."* He frequently wept like a child and exclaimed, *"I alone have, for a moment, been set at liberty; but six of our comrades are still lingering in confinement. I fear that, if I do not return speedily, they will be ill-treated by the Japanese."*

So much for our kind-hearted but stupid messenger. I relied however on Kahei's honesty as on a rock, and regarded all further precaution as superfluous. Golownin's letter merely to more completely inform us of what was required by the Japanese government, and this was in all events highly important.

Having satisfied our curiosity concerning the situation of our comrades, by a thousand various questions, we again put our friends Kahei and Simanoff ashore. I asked Kahei to inform Takahashi-Sampei that, should the wind prove favorable, I intended to set sail for Okhotsk on the following day, and that I would return to Hakodate in this year without fail, provided with all the documents he required; moreover, I begged that Kahei would offer him our sincere thanks for the friendly disposition he manifested, and particularly for permitting us an interview with our countryman.

Finally, on July 29, we took farewell of Takataya-Kahei. On this occasion, he brought three hundred fish on board for the sailors. I was somewhat mortified at his having constantly refused to accept any presents, except a little sugar, tea, and vodka. He even proposed that his clothes and other articles of property, which he had on board the *Diana*, and they were apparently of considerable value, should remain in my custody, observing that we should soon meet again in Hakodate. He said, *"There, I can without any obstruction receive the tokens of your friendship, but here it would be extremely troublesome to me to be made accountable, according to our laws, for every trifle."* I said, *"At least take back your own properties. You know the dangers involved in sea life at every moment."*

He exclaimed, *"How can you apprehend danger after the evident protection of Heaven you have experienced! CHEESAI, CHEESAI, TAISHO! (Small, small, commander!) You have sufficient time for accomplishing a safe voyage, a wise man like you who knows how to observe the TEN (a planet in the sky) cannot deny. It cannot fail. I don't like the way you look on your face. I see that you are concerned about my trifles, though it was my intention to request permission to distribute them among your seamen but I perceive your uneasiness of mind, which probably derives from your doubt on the negotiations being finally adjusted within this year. Consequently, I must conclude that your sailors, several of whom still distrust me, would imagine that I gave them presents under the conviction that I should never see them again. Therefore, I beg the trifles may remain in your hand until you return to Hakodate. TEN TAISHO! TEN signifies a place which restores confidence in God!"*

The penetrating and grateful Takataya-Kahei was indeed not wrong in his conjecture. But the reader may judge how great was our causes for uneasiness. As soon as he departed, we weighed anchor despite the unfavorable state of the weather, with the intention of heading into the sea. The wind soon became fair, and after a pleasant voyage of fifteen days, we again cast anchor in the Okhotsk harbor.

I immediately addressed a report to the commandant of Okhotsk containing an account of all that took place and he in return furnished me with the document required by the Japanese Government, together with a letter of friendly explanation from the governor of Irkutzk to the Matsumae bugyo which stated everything necessary.

A Japanese, named Kisseleff, who had been sent from Irkutzk to serve as our interpreter, now came on board the *Diana*. We remained in Okhotsk for eighteen days in order to bring aboard every supply we required for repairing the vessel, which had suffered considerable damage.

—The Third Voyage —

On August 11, we were ready to sail, for the third time, to the coast of Japan, with a full reliance on the assistance of Heaven in the attainment of our desired object. Before our departure we held solemn worship on board the vessel, and fired all our guns in honor of the Emperor.

Although at that moment the monarch was occupied with important affairs of Europe, he did not forget his few unfortunate subjects. He ordered an expedition for the liberation of Captain Golownin at this port, ten thousand wersts away from his capital.

Among the visitors to come on board the *Diana*, were the Commandant of the harbor, Minitzky, and his amiable wife, Eugenia Nikolanona. The warm wishes this lady entertained for our success, induced her to venture onto those stormy roads where her husband had nearly lost his life during the previous year at the same season. She was the only Russian lady who honored the *Diana* with a visit, and she is therefore entitled to the sincere thanks, which together with the rest of the officers, I took this opportunity to offer her. During the worship the motion of the ship was so violent that all our guests from the shore, with the exception of this youthful heroine, were seized with sickness. She devoutly joined us in prayer for the liberation of our comrades.

Owing to the adverse southerly winds that prevailed along the Peninsula of Sakhalin, twenty days elapsed before we reached the coast of Matsumae. On September 10, we entered <u>Vulcano Bay</u>, where the safe harbor of <u>Etomo</u> is situated, and at once resolved to repair. As we approached the promontory, we could plainly observe the buildings and even the inhabitants of the place.

With six hours of favorable wind we expected to reach the harbor; but there is no certainty at sea. During the night the wind became more adverse than before, and a storm arose and remained a while, which on the following morning drove us from the coast. It was at the period of the equinox when in this part of the world, violent storms prevail even more frequently than elsewhere. It now appeared doubtful that we would be able to reach the Japanese coasts this autumn.

In this case I determined to proceed to the <u>Sandwich Islands</u> instead of returning to Kamchatka.

This would entail a great loss of time because the long winter would require us to lie there three months and return by the month of April when the navigation on the northern coasts of Japan would be open again. I conveyed this plan to the rest of the officers, though I did not wish to carry it into effect until October 1.

In furtherance of the plan, it was necessary for the crew to submit without a murmur, but to our great joy, the storm abated on the twelfth day, and, as is usual with seamen, mild and favorable breezes soon made us forget all our past sufferings.

One melancholy circumstance, however, occurred to interrupt our happiness. We had the misfortune to lose one of our bravest and most experienced sailors. This poor man met with a severe accident among the rigging, and on being brought down, all surgical aid proved ineffectual. At such a moment it would perhaps have been advantageous if our surgeon could have gone aloft. Unfortunately he had served only in the army and was unaccustomed to climbing the shrouds, though he was in other respects an extremely active and courageous man.

He was not the same surgeon whom we had brought with us from Kronstadt. That officer had, on account of ill health, returned Petersburg.

In our situation we felt, with double severity, the loss of this valuable seaman. As we committed our sailor's body to the waves with due religious solemnity, the whole crew melted into tears—a spontaneous tribute paid to his six years of faithful service.

What service! The reader must be aware that our path was not strewn with roses. Only people who have been in a similar situation can conceive how close the knot of friendship is drawn when it is united together by a little strand among people separated from their friends and relatives for a long time.

When we entered Vulcano Bay on October 22 at nine in the morning, three baidares were observed steering toward our vessel. I dispatched Lieutenant Filatoff to meet them, and he soon conducted them alongside. There were eighteen Japanese on board these baidares, who boldly ascended the deck of the *Diana* at our invitation.

We inquired where we could find a harbor, and they informed us there was one called <u>Sawara</u>, about two wersts distant, in a southerly direction, near the promontory, which had about twenty fathoms depth of water. We soon found they came on board merely from curiosity to see the foreign ship. We wished to moor at Etomo where Captain Broughton had visited in 1796. We requested them to show us to the port, but they declined. Probably because they were out here without permission, and left us.

From Captain Broughton's description, we

were, however, fairly certain of being able to enter the harbor without their assistance, and we accordingly stood into it with an easterly wind. At noon, we discovered a tolerably large village, and on the heights batteries that were overhung with cloth. A baidare was sent out to meet us. Thirteen hairy Kuriles were on board whom Japanese called <u>Ainu</u>. These Kuriles were accompanied by a native Japanese, named <u>Heizo</u>, who had been in Kamchatka with Takataya-Kahei. We put him ashore on our return to Kunashiri. He informed us that in consequence of the agreement concluded at Kunashiri, he was sent by the Matsumae bugyo as a pilot to conduct us to the harbor of Hakodate.

He inquired whether we wanted anything. He told us the authorities of that place had been directed to furnish us with whatever we might require. We stood in need of nothing except fresh water, and I availed myself of the opportunity to send fifty empty casks to shore. We then cast anchor in eleven fathoms with a muddy bottom.

On the following day, the same baidare, manned by the same Kuriles, brought back our casks filled with fresh water from Etomo, and likewise some fresh fish and radishes as presents from the governor. We returned him our thanks and again sent twenty empty casks, which were brought back in the evening.

We took advantage of the fine weather to repair our rigging, which was considerably damaged during the storm, and everything was soon restored to a state of good order. For several days the Japanese continued to fill our casks, and to send presents of fresh fish and vegetables in such abundance as enabled us to deal out plentiful supplies to the crew. In spite of all our persuasions, the Japanese obstinately refused to accept anything in return.

On the morning of the twenty-sixth, the baidare brought me a letter from Captain Golownin written in Hakodate. He informed me that when the *Diana* should come within sight of the harbor, a white flag would be displayed on the hill and Takataya-Kahei would be sent out to us. Because Kahei could not depart without an order from the Matsumae bugyo, Captain Golownin advised us, in the meanwhile, to trust to the sailor Heizo, who was a skillful pilot. This letter was reply to one I addressed to the Japanese authorities upon our first arrival at Etomo, in which I expressed my doubts regarding the sincerity of the Japanese, since they sent a common sailor to meet us, instead of dispatching Takataya-Kahei or some individual of rank. Now, however, I was very willing to accept Heizo as pilot.

Without any trouble, we got all our empty casks filled with fresh water and every other necessary supply. We set sail at ten o'clock. At eight o'clock on the following evening, we discovered fires along various parts of Matsumae coast. One of these was particularly large and blazing. We were soon met by a baidare, bearing a white flag and two lanterns. Our faithful friend Takataya-Kahei was on board. This proved to be a joyful meeting for both parties.

There was now every probability of our mutual wishes being fulfilled. He came by the order of Japanese government to conduct us into the harbor of Hakodate. He was himself accompanied by a distinguished officer of the port. By their mutual direction we cast anchor at half past eight in the evening, at a spot called *Yamase-Tomari* by the Japanese. It was a common anchoring place for the vessels when easterly winds prevented them from entering the harbor.

When every necessary arrangement was made, we eagerly sat down to converse with the good Kahei, with whom we communicated with more facility than before, because we had interpreter Kesseleff for assistance.

Our first question was, of course, related to our comrades. Kahei informed us that they were in Hakodate, and that the Matsumae Bugyo, Hattori-Bingono-Kami, had already arrived in person for the purpose of concluding the negotiation and liberating the prisoner. We conversed together for a considerable time, and I gave an account of the total overthrow of the <u>French</u>, to which he listened with unfeigned interest. He then took his leave, promising he would return next day to conduct the ship into the harbor. During the night, we observed fires burning along various parts of the coast, and a watch-boat rowed up to us and lay near the vessel as long as we remained there.

Kahei fulfilled his promise of returning early on the following morning. We sailed into the Bay of Hakodate, and after a few hours, we cast anchor in a place he pointed out to us, which was scarcely the distance of a gunshot from the city. He then acquainted me with the laws concerning European vessels. He stated that we could not be permitted to sail about the harbor in boats. As long as we remained there, a watch-boat would, day and night, be stationed near the vessel and everything we stood in need of would be conveyed to us by government vessels; all persons were strictly prohibited from visiting us. In the evening, Kahei went on shore in order to draw up a circumstantial report of his proceedings.

The city of Hakodate, the second in magnitude on the island, is situated on the island's southern coast, on the declivity of a high circular hill, which rises above the peninsula there formed. It is washed on the south by the strait of Tsugaru, and on the north and west by the Bay of Hakodate. This situation was very convenient for receiving a large fleet. The peninsula forms its junction on the east by a narrow land bridge so that there is at once a view of both the open sea and the low grounds.

On the northern side of the bay, a spacious valley extends over a circuit of fifteen or twenty miles, bounded on three of its sides by hills. In the center of this valley lies the village of Oono, the inhabitants of which are chiefly occupied in agriculture. The other villages situated on the coast are, for the most part, inhabited by fishermen.

We learned these particulars from our friends upon their return, for they had conducted about the city, and on their walks observed that this valley was better cultivated than any other district they had seen. The city is built at the foot of a valley, and serves as an excellent landmark for ships entering the bay. It is easily recognized at a distance by its circular form, and is detached from every other elevated object.

On the western side, this hill is formed of huge masses of rock, in one of which there is a cavity perceptible from the sea. The depth of water, close to land, is quite substantial on the southern and western sides of the peninsula, but as there are neither sandbanks nor rocks to be apprehended, the coast may be approached without danger. There are, however, numerous sandbanks on the northern side, and consequently only small vessels can reach the village. From the projecting cape opposite the village, a sandbank of unequal depth extends one-third of the breadth of the bay. On the northern and eastern sides of the bay, the depth of the water gradually diminishes toward the shore.

As we approached the village, we observed that cloth was hung out only at a few places on the hill, or near it, and not over the whole buildings as at Kunashiri. With the assistance of our telescope, we observed six of these screens of cloth, probably destined to conceal fortifications, which our comrades had an opportunity of seeing on their way from Matsumae to Hakodate. There were, besides, five new fortifications erected along the coast, and provided with garrisons of suitable strength; they stood at short distances from one another, and about from two to three hundred fathoms from the shore.

We no sooner entered the roads than we were surrounded by a number of boats of all descriptions and sizes, filled with the curious of both sexes. A European ship must, indeed, have been to them an object of uncommon interest; for, as far as I could ascertain, they had seen none since they were visited twenty-two years ago by Laxman, and Lowzoff, the commander of the Okhotsk transport ship *Catharina*. Many of the inhabitants, therefore, had never beheld a European vessel of any kind, and still less a ship of war; they accordingly thronged around us in vast numbers, and their curiosity frequently gave rise to disputes among themselves.

The doshin (police force) on the watch boats continually warned them to keep at farther distance. People generally show great respect to the doshin but the confusion was so great that their orders were, on this occasion, disregarded. The doshin were, therefore, forced to use their iron clubs, which they carried fastened around their waist by a long silken belt.

They spared neither rank nor sex; old persons alone experienced their indulgence. We had various opportunities of observing that the Japanese, in all situations, pay particular respect to old age. In this case, blows were freely dealt out to the young of every description who ventured to disobey the commands of the soldiers. We were at length delivered from a multitude of visitors who would have subjected us to no small degree of inconvenience. We should have been unable to move had they all been permitted to come on board the vessel and to keep them out by force was a measure which we could not have adopted without reluctance, considering the favorable turn which our intercourse with the Japanese had taken.

They were at last, however, compelled to withdraw to a certain distance indicated by the guards, and no boats dared to pass the boundary. In this manner they covered a considerable portion of the bay, and when those who were most ahead had gratified their curiosities, the places were immediately occupied by the next in succession. They did not all depart until twilight; after which only those individuals who were sent by the government were allowed to approach our ship, and even they were subject to the examination of the watch boat.

Next morning, we observed a boat bearing a white flag standing toward us from the village. Takataya-Kahei, with the sailor who had been our pilot, came on board in this boat, and brought presents of fish, vegetables, and water-melons. The sailor carried a bundle, which I perceived contained clothes. Kahei begged that I would permit him to retire to his old cabin to dress, informing me that the Matsumae bugyo, who was highly satisfied with his services in Kunashiri, had appointed him negotiator in this important affair, on which occasion he had, according to the customs of Japan, been invested with certain privileges.

In fulfillment of this duty, it was necessary that, during his communications with me, he should appear in the robes appropriate to his official situation. He accordingly withdrew, to attire himself, and in the meanwhile I put on my state uniform and hung my sword by my side. After a polite salutation, Kahei intimated through our interpreter Kisseleff that he did not now speak in the name of the bugyo, but rather in the name of the two chief officers, who requested that I would deliver the official paper I had been engaged to bring from Okhotsk.

I replied that I was prepared to present it to the officers themselves, but in order that no time might be lost I would deliver it to Kahei. I assembled my officers in full uniform, in the cabin, to witness this proceeding, and with all due solemnity I presented to Kahei the official document from the Commandant of Okhotsk, which was wrapped in blue cloth. At the same time, I stated that I had, in my possession, another important official letter from His Excellency the governor of Irkutzk to the most powerful Matsumae bugyo, but which I could deliver only in person, either to the bugyo or to some distinguished officer who might be sent to receive it. Takataya-Kahei urgently asked that I give him this letter also, as it would procure him high honor in Japan when it should be known that he was thought worthy of delivering into the hand of the bugyo an official document from the Russian governor. I resolutely declined this request, observing that, though I loved him as a friend, I could not consent to anything that might be considered derogatory to the dignity of the governor of Irkutzk, nor betray the trust he placed in me.

I now proposed that my interview with the Japanese authorities should take place on shore but close to the sea, as I found it was impractical to communicate with them in boat. According to Kahei, people in the streets sit upon their knees whenever the two chief officers appeared in their *norimon* (carriage). How then could we hope that they would consent to lay aside all their ceremonies and hold a conference in boats with the commander of a foreign ship! Besides, I had credentials from the governor of Irkutzk.

I was invested with full powers in conformity with the pleasure of my sovereign, and consequently appeared in the character of ambassador. Therefore, if the Japanese dared to act treacherously, I was certain my treatment would not be looked upon with indifference, but would be considered as a national concern. I had also less reason to hesitate in fulfilling my mission in the usual manner, as I knew that the dignity of an ambassador was much respected in Japan.

Takataya-Kahei begged that I would think

no more about his indiscreet request, and then went ashore. He returned next day, dressed himself as before, and in the name of the two principal officers, inquired whether the crew of the *Diana* stood in need of anything, or whether the ship itself required repair, as she probably suffered damage during her long voyage, at that late season of the year. I returned my thanks, and observed that we had a good supply of everything, except fresh water, fish, and vegetables, all of which abounded in Hakodate, and that the ship was in a state of perfect repair.

Kahei then informed me that he had delivered the official document, from the commandant of Okhotsk, with all due ceremonies; its contents were deemed satisfactory, and my proposal to hold an interview with the commandant, in order to present the letter from the governor of Irkutzk, had been accepted. He added that the object of his present visit was to arrange the ceremonies it would be necessary to observe during this conference. To start with, he wanted to settle matters regarding the guard of honor. I reported that I would bring ten men with me on shore, armed with muskets; two petty officers should precede me, carrying the war-flag and the white flag of truce; and I should be accompanied by two commissioned officers and the interpreter.

Besides this, I consented to be rowed ashore

in the governor's state barge. After mutual salutation, which on my side was to be made in the European manner, by a bow, an arm chair was to be placed for me, and behind it two common chairs for my officers. During the introductory address whether it proceeded from the Japanese or myself, I was, as a mark of respect, to stand and then immediately to take my seat. With the exception of the muskets, Kahei observed that all these regulations would be readily agreed.

He said, *"But we know of no instance in which a foreign ambassador, whatever might be the object of his mission to Japan, has been suffered to present himself at a ceremonial conference with a retinue bearing firearms. Be satisfied with the same mark of respect that has been shown to other European ambassadors in Nagasaki; namely, the men dressed in your suit shall be permitted to wear their swords, but let them leave their muskets behind them. Instead, allow your ship to sail into the inner-most harbor, and to arm and provide with powder. This will leave you the means of reacting against us if you please, though these are by no means a deviation from our laws."*

As I was well convinced that favors had been conceded to us that no other European ship had ever enjoyed, I was prepared to yield the point with respect to the muskets. I merely observed to Kahei that a guard without muskets was not a guard of war, and was consequently beneath my rank as commander of a Russian imperial ship.

I said, *"According to our tradition, only men in the military and naval service are permitted to carry muskets, in the same manner as such persons wear two sabres in Japan. Our muskets therefore correspond exactly with your two sabres."*

I added that if this proposition were objectionable, he need not insist upon it, and I would go on shore upon the other conditions being agreed. Having made memorandums of all that passed between us, he took his leave.

On the following day he came with a joyful countenance, to inform me that everything was settled even the point regarding the muskets.

He said, *"At first, our officers were all silent, but after they had considered the matter for some time, I repeated all your arguments, one after another. I am now directed to inform you that the two first officers will expect you tomorrow, at the place appointed on the shore, to receive the letter from the governor of Irkutzk from your hands. At twelve o'clock the governor's state-barge will be ready to receive you.*

One thing only remains to be arranged that you may on no account appear in boots in the audience-chamber, which is covered with fine carpets. High-ranking officers will sit with folded legs. To appear there in boots would be quite repugnant to our customs, and the most unwarrantable indecorum. You must consequently leave your boots in the chamber, and enter only in your socks."

I was somewhat embarrassed by this singular proposal, which was so opposed to every European notion of propriety. In making arrangements for the ceremonies, I had never once thought of mentioning my boots.

The Japanese, on the other hand, likewise thought it superfluous to say a word on the subject, for as Captain Golownin afterward informed me, their demand referred merely to a common act of politeness. I replied with some degree of warmth, that I would never consent to appear in full uniform with a sword by my side and without either boots or shoes. I observed to Kahei that I was well aware it was customary with the Japanese to take off their shoes even before they enter a common apartment.

I said, *"But you are an intelligent man, and cannot but know how widely your customs differ from those of European nations. Your comrades, for instance, instead of trousers, wear a loose address resembling our night-gowns, and in which no European gentleman would tolerate himself to be*

110

seen, except in his bed-chamber. You never enter a strange house with your shoes on and on the same token wherever you go barefoot would with us be esteemed rude and even disgraceful, and only befitting the lowest of criminals. How can you expect that a man of my rank should comply with such customs?"

Takataya-Kahei could make no reply; he had never bestowed a moment's thought on this important point. I reflected for a few moments, and then declared that I should endeavor to comply with all that was required, in order that no obstacle might stand in the way of the proposed conference.

I continued, *"In Russia, it is customary, when we wish to show particular respect to any person of distinction, to exchange our boots for shoes in the anti-chamber."*

Kahei exclaimed joyfully, *"That is sufficient. No violation of the rules of politeness need be made by either party. Your shoes may easily be compared to our Japanese tabi and I will say that you agree to take off your boots, and to appear in the audience-chamber in leather socks."*

He immediately went ashore, and to my astonishment returned in the evening to inform me that the officers were highly satisfied with my arrangement regarding the leather socks. He added that if, however, I absolutely insisted on appearing in boots I might do so. This would be allowed even though the officers, instead of receiving me on their knees, must sit on chairs after the European manner, which in Japan is regarded as a great disrespect and even rudeness.

He then produced a drawing of the building and proposed where the interview should take place. In front of the edifice, a number of soldiers were sketched, sitting with folded legs. In the first apartment, the officers of inferior rank were assigned. Here I was to draw off my boots, and then pass by a row of officers likewise sitting with folded legs.

At the upper end of the hall of audience, the places for the two chief officers were marked out. On the left the interpreter, on the right an academician who arrived for the express purpose of making observations on the Russian war ship and collecting particulars for European sciences. My place was marked out in the center of the hall, facing the high authorities, and behind me were chairs for my two officers. The guards with muskets and flags were sketched in front of the open doors of the building.

Everything being thus arranged, Kahei took his leave, promising if the weather should prove favorable, to return at twelve o'clock the next day to escort me in the state barge. I now turned my thoughts to our interpreter, Kisseleff, whom it was necessary I should take ashore along with me. I was well aware of the severity of the laws of Japan toward subjects who have become Christians and lived in foreign countries.

Kisseleff, in the letter he translated, had described himself to be a native of Russia, though the son of a Japanese woman. Yet it appeared probable that his perfect knowledge of the Japanese language would immediately betray him and in that case, the consequences might be fatal. I left it to his own free choice whether or not he would incur the danger.

He replied, *"What have I to fear? If they detain you, they detain us all. They will not seize me alone. I am not Japanese, so do not treat me any differently. Take me with you, so that I might have an opportunity to fulfill my duty. The conference will be of the highest importance, but I can be of no service to you by remaining on board the ship. For what purpose did I encounter the danger of this long voyage, if I am now to be left behind?"*

I gladly consented to take him with me and I gave orders that the two officers who of their own accord offered to accompany me should hold themselves in readiness.

Next day, at twelve o'clock, the state barge was sent out with a number of flags waving on board.

Takataya-Kahei appeared in full costume, and informed me that we should depart whenever the flag was displayed from the building. In accordance with this, the conference was to take place. The flag was unfurled precisely at twelve o'clock, and we went on board the barge. The barge was rowed by sixteen specially chosen Japanese. Most of them, Kahei informed me, were eminent and wealthy merchants who had seized this opportunity of gratify their curiosity.

Their manner of rowing differs from the European. In this, they do not throw the blade of the oar forward, but keep merely turning it about and yet the boat is moved with as much velocity as would be produced by our method. We fixed our war flag alongside the Japanese flags in the stern at the prow. We also however, hoisted the white flag of truce, and in this manner we rowed toward the village, accompanied by several hundred boats filled with spectators. The building in which the conference was to take place was situated close to the shore, near a stone landing place.

In the front of the house we observed a number of Japanese soldiers sitting on the ground in accordance with their custom. Takataya-Kahei was first to step out of the barge. He proceeded immediately to the house, to inform the high officers of our arrival, and soon returned to intimate that everything was prepared for our reception. To have enquired why no Japanese officer had been dispatched to meet me seemed then to be an untimely and useless question.

I therefore ordered the petty officer, who was the bearer of the white flag, to land next to the ten marines under arms, and the other petty officer to follow with the war flag. Then, I stepped out of the barge followed by two commissioned officers. The marines arranged themselves in front of the open doors, and saluted me in the military style as I passed. In the entrance hall, my shoes were put on by Japanese attendants and one of them carried a chair behind me. I then entered the audience-chamber, which was filled with the officers of various ranks, all wearing their military dresses and two sabres.

I was somewhat surprised at the dead silence that prevailed throughout the apartment. On observing the two chief officers who were sitting near each other with folded legs, I advanced toward them and bowed. They returned my salutation by an inclination of the head. I then bowed to the right and left, and took my seat in the chair that had been placed for me. Uninterrupted silence prevailed for several minutes. I was the first to break it by observing through the interpreter Kisseleff that I considered myself to be in the presence of friends. Instead of making any reply, the two chief officers laughed, but the elder of the two, who had come from Kunashiri, opened the conference by turning to an officer who sat on his left. While he spoke, he inclined his head toward the ground, but spoke in so low a tone of voice that Kisseleff could not collect a word he said.

The officer who listened in the manner I described resumed his former attitude after a respectful salutation. To my great astonishment, he addressed me in tolerably good Russian. He was, as I afterward learned, the interpreter Murakami-Teisuke, who had been taught Russian by Captain Golownin. He said, *"The Russians, some time ago, occasioned great disturbances on the coasts of Japan, but all is now happily settled. The certificate of the Natschalnik of Okhotsk is very, very satisfactory."*

I answered, *"through him as interpreter that by the happy settlement of which he spoke the liberation of our prisoners was doubtless to be understood. This, for our part, would repay all the hardships we had endured for this day of joy."*

After some interchange of compliments, I proceeded to call the attention of the superior officers to the letter of the governor of Irkutzk, which Savelieff handed to me in a box covered with a purple cloth. I took it out and read the address aloud and returned it.

Savelieff replaced the letter, and handed the box to the interpreter, who elevated it above his head, and placed it in the hands of the junior of the two great officers. The latter raised it to the height of his breast, and delivered it to the senior officer, who stated that he would immediately present it to the bugyo. In consideration of the importance of the document, he said, *"Two days would be necessary for preparing the answer."*

Our presents were handed by Savelieff to the Japanese interpreter, who laid them before the officers. They both requested that I would accept of some refreshments, which were prepared in the house. They stood up and bowed toward me and withdrew with the presents. The interpreter Murakami-Teisuke, then welcomed us in a very friendly manner, addressed me by my Russian name, and said, *"God blessed us! I can now congratulate you on a happy settlement. Captain Golownin and the other Russians will soon be sent on board to you. Our laws do not permit that you should yet meet, but they are all well."*

The Academician also congratulated us and our worthy friend Takataya-Kahei who during the ceremony had stood at the extremity of the chamber and now approached. We were treated with tea and sweetmeats served on lacquered trays.

I was distinguished by having an officer of

subaltern rank placed by my side. He received whatever was destined for me and presented it. After having been on shore two hours, we took leave and returned on board with Kahei.

I ordered Lieutenant Filatoff to decorate the ship with flags as soon as he saw us land but not to fire, for I knew that the Japanese would not be pleased with that compliment. Unlike Europeans, they regard the firing of cannons, which are engines of destruction, as an absurd mark of honor and respect. There are, however, instances of the practice among themselves. The governor of Sendai, for example, is saluted with rounds of artillery upon leaving or entering his principality.

The day was fine, and the decoration of the ship with flags afforded a delightful spectacle to the curious of both sexes, who crowded out in boats to view it. Thus it ended, to the satisfaction of both parties our conference with the Japanese authorities. During all this time, the Russian imperial flag waved for the first time on the territory of this haughty people and received due honors. The escorts who accompanied me had sworn not to allow the sacred imperial standard to pass from their hands while one of them remained alive.

We must again gratefully acknowledge that the enlightened and generous Takataya-Kahei was on this occasion a great gift to us. Two days passed away without any communications from the high authorities. During this time, Kahei visited us twice a day accompanied by some of his friends the government gave him permission to bring on board. These visits were extremely agreeable to us, as they afforded us an opportunity to testify to Kahei how much we considered ourselves obliged to him. We offered his friends presents, but they would accept only some trifles, and not even a small part of them without Kahei's permission.

On the morning of the third day, Kahei came on board, with his countenance sparkling with joy, to inform me that I might have a conference with Captain Golownin and the other Russian prisoners. What a joyful message, despite the fact we received only short notes of acknowledgement in return for the receipt of our letters. This plainly proved that the Japanese inspected what he wrote, and thus obliged him to observe great caution on his correspondence. Toward evening, Takataya-Kahei brought us an irrefragable proof of meeting our friends: namely, a letter from Captain Golownin expressed satisfaction at being introduced to his acquaintance.

On the following day, Kahei thrilled me with the intimation that I might go on shore that day, and would find my friend Golownin and two of his sailors

119

in the same edifice where the solemn conference with the Japanese authorities had been held.

The interpreter Murakami-Teisuke, the academician, and some officers of inferior rank, were to be present at this meeting. The governor's barge was to convey me onshore, and I was at liberty to take with me the same number of armed men as on the first occasion. With regard to the last suggestion, I answered that as this was to be merely a private interview, I would leave the two flags in the boat, and only take onshore with me the ship's clerk and five unarmed sailors, in order that they could enjoy the pleasure of seeing two of their old shipmates.

Next morning at ten o'clock, Kahei came to me, and I went on shore with him and the men I promised to take in the governor's barge. As we approached the shore, I saw Golownin at the door of the edifice in a rich yellow dress with his sword by his side. I instantly forgot all attention to ceremony and did not allow Takataya-Kahei to precede me, but leaped first on shore myself. I had served so long with Golownin, and lived in the intimate friendship, that I certainly should easily recognize him in his habiliments. I was uncertain, however, among a crowd of Japanese and the joy of our first embrace may be imagined, but cannot be described. He had almost ceased to hope to see his country again, and I scarcely ventured to hope that it would fall to my lot to deliver him. Now, however, we were locked in each other's arms. The delicacy of the Japanese made them desirous not to disturb the transport of our feelings. They accordingly drew back and chatted to each other.

At first we could only express ourselves in unconnected questions and answers, but when we became somewhat tranquil we spoke on the main object of our meeting, for which sufficient time was allowed us. Golownin, in a few words, related what he suffered and in return required from me an account of the situation of his country, his friends, and his relatives. He then showed me that I formed an erroneous opinion on a very important point.

The poor condition of the ship induced me to cherish the idea of wintering in Hakodate, as it appeared hazardous to return to Kamchatka at that late period of the year. Golownin however, observed that according to the Japanese laws, we would be considered prisoners and that it was therefore necessary to hasten our departure. On his advice, I wrote to that effect to the Japanese authorities. We took leave of each other, full of the hope of speedily meeting, never to be again so separated.

In the evening I had the pleasure of a visit from Kahei. He had been present at my interview with Golownin, but in the midst of it he came up to me and said, *"I am not well—excuse me,"* and went away.

The sailors who accompanied me, and who never could place any faith in the Japanese, were alarmed at Kahei's withdrawing, particularly as in passing he had told them farewell in a very serious manner. They firmly believed that the Japanese were going to arrest me.

On this occasion, Kahei brought a youth on board with him, and intimated that he had something wonderful to tell me. Yesterday, on the way returning home, he said, very unexpectedly he found the young man. He wanted me to guess who he was. It was his son! Kahei said, *"Look at him! Isn't he like me? I received the most joyful information of my wife from him. She returned from her pilgrimage in good health, and she scarcely entered her home, scarcely laid aside her travelling dress, when she received the letter via courier I wrote to her on our arrival at Kunashiri."*

I expressed a sincere wish for the future happiness of my friend and his affectionate wife. These events confirmed him still more in his belief of predestination to which he was much devoted. I paid particular attention to his son and ordered that he should be shown every part of the ship, and introduced him to my officers who, with assistance of Kesseleff, carried on a friendly conversation. In the meantime Kahei told me about his friend in the hermitage.

He said, *"Taisho! Men are to be found in Japan without the help of the <u>lantern.</u> How do you think I can make a return to my friend? He despises riches. I must do something worthy of his greatness of soul. You know I have a daughter, but owing to her misconduct, I have forbidden her to bear my name. It's been long since I shut her out and regarded her as if she has been dead. You have taken a great interest in her fate; I have always been deeply moved whenever you entreated that I would become reconciled to her. Perhaps you thought your friendship slighted because I remained inexorable, but you knew not the customs of our country, nor were you aware that you required a sacrifice of my honor."*

He continued, *"Now! Since I possess so invaluable a treasure in my friend, who has withdrawn himself from the world, I will make a sacrifice as rare as his friendship. A sacrifice that according to our idea of honor, is the severest wound that the heart of a father can endure. I have resolved to call my daughter into life, and to forgive her. I need only communicate this determination to my friend, and he will understand me."*

He then requested I would permit him to distribute the properties he had on board the ship among the seamen. This he did in person, giving articles of highest value to such crew as he was best acquainted with, particularly our cook, whom Kahei used to call his friend for he honored my dishes of morality with the title of Kusuri (medicine). Yet he was not insensible that he needed food for the body as well as the mind, and the former was also kusuri to him. The articles he gave away consisted of silk and cotton dresses, large wadded quilts, and nightgowns. These were so numerous that every man on board received a present of some kind or other. Then, he requested that the sailors might be allowed to make that evening merry.

He said, *"Taisho! Sailors are all alike, whether Russian or Japanese. They are all fond of sake and there is no danger in the harbor of Hakodate."*

Though I had, on that joyful day, already ordered a double allowance of grog to be served out to the crew. I could not decline complying with the request of the good Kahei. He immediately sent his sailors on shore to procure sake and, according to the Japanese custom, ordered them to bring pipes of tobacco for each of our seamen. I conducted him to the cabin, where I had previously laid out the presents that had been sent with the embassy. They consisted of painted porcelain, marble slabs and crystal vessels of various descriptions. I said, *"Now, fulfill the promise that you made in Kunashiri. Take whatever you like best. Or, since your officers despise our presents, take them all to yourself."*

With all the sincerity of friendship, he said,

"To what purpose should I accept of the costly things? According to our laws, they must all be taken from me, and the government will merely indemnify me with money."

With considerable difficulties, I prevailed on him to accept of a few trifles. He chose what pleased him best, namely a pair of silver spoons, two knives and other articles for the table. He was particularly delighted, however, on my presenting him with a tea service. He said, *"I can now entertain my friends with the Russian style in remembrance of the hospitality I have experienced with you."*

In general he expressed himself pleased with our mode of living. Although he could not always sit at table with us, because the Japanese do not eat butchers' meat, he had his meals served at the same time, and always took tea with us. He generally drank his tea without sugar, but he ate large quantities of the latter separately.

We remained together until midnight. When about to withdraw he expressed his regret that the Japanese laws did not allow him to invite and entertain us at his own house, for there we might possess some <u>hashi</u> and <u>sakazuki,</u> as a memory of Japanese hospitality.

On the following day, we were much concerned to hear that Takataya-Kahei had caught a severe cold, in consequence of his frequent communications with the *Diana* which obliged him to be so much on the water. We were visited instead by the younger interpreter, who was sent by the high officers to inform us that on the following morning Golownin and the rest of the prisoners would be sent on board. In confirmation of this message, he brought a letter from Golownin. It appeared that they had all been carried before the bugyo and in the presence of a numerous assembly he had formally announced their liberation. The high officers requested that next morning I would go once more on shore, to hold a conference with them to take charge of my liberated comrades, and to receive the papers that had been prepared for me.

As proof that I implicitly relied on the honor of the Japanese government, I informed our welcome messenger that I would go ashore without guards, and merely in a boat bearing white flags in order to convince the people that the liberation of our comrades had been effected without any use of force whatever. The interpreter, along with some other visitors who were attracted by curiosity, remained with us until night, and we now for the first time succeeded in persuading our guests to receive a few tokens of friendship. Our presents on this occasion consisted of pieces of Spanish leather, which the Japanese prized beyond anything else we could have offered them.

October 7 was a happy day. On this day all our difficulties were to be amply requited. Takataya-Kahei arrived very early in the governor's barge. Owing to indisposition he appeared in his ordinary dress. Upon my expressing some apprehensions on account of his health, he replied, *"Never fear! Joy has already made me better, and when I see you and Golownin rowing toward the ship, I shall be quite well again."* He assured us that the bugyo was much pleased with the frank confidence I had placed in the honor of the Japanese. At twelve o'clock, I went on board the barge, accompanied only by Savelieff and Kisseleff, and rowed under white flags to the well-known edifice where the Japanese waited to receive us.

Our prisoners immediately appeared at the door. They all wore yellow dresses of a uniform cut, with seamen's trousers and waistcoats of various colors. The officers' dresses were made of a material resembling our figured silk stuffs, those of the sailors consisted of taffeta. The Kurile, Alexei, wore a dress of dark-colored silk, made in the Japanese form.

To complete this whimsical costume, the officers wore their sabres and uniform hats. On any other occasion, we should have been highly diverted by the singularity of their appearance, but now it did not even excite a smile. Friend gazed at friend with emotion and joy, and our thoughts were expressed more by our looks than by words.

Tears of gratitude to Providence glistened in the eyes of our liberated comrades. The Japanese retired and left us for some time alone, in order that we might give vent to our feelings. My comrades were then formally delivered over to me by the two Ginmiyaku Takahashi-Sampei and Kujimoto-Hyogoro. The papers of the Japanese government, which I was to lay before the authorities upon my arrival in Russia, were presented to me according to the ceremonies that have already been described by Captain Golownin. Refreshments were then handed to us in the usual manner.

Having once more expressed our sincere thanks, we rowed away from the shore at two o'clock, accompanied by a countless number of boats, crowded with Japanese men and women. Despite a violent adverse wind, none of the numerous boats by which we were surrounded pushed back. The *Diana* was decorated with flags, and all the yards were manned by the crew who saluted us with three cheers. The enthusiasm of the seamen, on once more beholding their beloved commander and his comrades in misfortune after a separation of two years and three months, was indeed boundless.

Many were moved to tears. This scene, so highly honorable to the whole crew, can never be effaced from my recollection. Golownin and his comrades, who were moved to their inmost souls, knelt down before the sacred image of the ship the miracle-working SAINT NICOLAS, and returned thanks to heaven.

A number of boats now came alongside, bringing fresh water, wood, one thousand large radishes, fifty boxes filled with grits, thirty with salt, and in short, provisions of every description though none had been requested on our part. When we declared that we stood in no need of these supplies, the Japanese replied that they had been ordered to provide the prisoners with provisions sufficient to last them until they reached Kamchatka. To avoid anything like dispute, I accepted everything that was sent.

A considerable time was spent in unloading the boats. Many of the Japanese, the doshin now permitted to come on board the vessel, set to work so zealously that it was difficult to say which most deserved admiration: the pleasure with which our seamen worked, or the obliging manner in which the Japanese assisted them.

They appeared as one people, and no spectator could have supposed that between their native homes half the circumference of the globe intervened! Civility, kindness, good humor and activity animated all. They reciprocally toasted each other with <u>vodka</u> and <u>sake</u>; and, in the midst of their labors, they enjoyed a holiday!

Some Japanese officers, of the rank of <u>Shitayaku</u>, came on board to visit us. Among them were interpreters, the Shitayaku Murakami-Teisuke and the <u>Zaiju-Kumajiro</u>. The former spoke Russian much better than the latter, and also possessed more general information. They were accompanied by the academician and an interpreter of the Dutch language, the latter of whom had been in Nagasaki when RESANOFF and KRUSENSTERN visited that port by the Nadeschda.

The Dutch interpreter recollected several of the Russian officer's names, and also spoke some Russian and understood French. We entertained them in the European style in the cabin and they examined every part of the ship with the greatest attention. Toward evening a multitude of Japanese came on board, but all were men, for now to our mortification, the women were not permitted to enter the ship.

The deck was so crowded that our seamen could not move a step without difficulty. The doshin were at last obliged to employ their iron clubs in driving people into the boats, whence the women looked anxiously up as if they wished to have a share in the bustle. To console them, we handed some trifles down to them, for which they returned thanks by very expressive gestures.

On October 10, when all was ready for our departure, the government sent us a quantity of vegetables along with fresh and salt fish. I had just given orders for weighing anchor when Takataya-Kahei appeared, with a number of boats, which he brought to tow us from the harbor into the bay.

The old interpreter and several of Golownin's acquaintances also came out in a large boat and accompanied us to the mouth of the bay. The ship's company took leave of our Japanese friends by cheering them. As a mark of sincere gratitude to Kahei, they called out, *"The Taisho! Hurrah!"* in three separate and additional cheers. Kahei and his sailors stood up in their boat and returned the cheers, calling as loud as they could, *"The Diana! Hurrah!"*

We had to contend with a heavy storm, of six

hours duration, along the Japanese coast. Our situation was extremely dangerous. The night was dark and the rain fell in a torrent. The water in the hold rose to forty inches, despite our effort keeping the pumps constantly at work. At last, the storm moderated, and in the midst of a shower of snow, we happily entered the harbor of Petropaulowski on the third of September.

On November 6, we held our last ceremony on board the ship, and proceeded to the barracks we had occupied during the preceding winter. We consoled ourselves with reflection that having now completed our labors, we should soon return to our friends and relatives, from whom we had been separated during the past seven years, or from the time we took our departure from Petersburg.

Thus we ended our first dialogue with the people who, through unfortunate circumstances and the misrepresentations of the selfish Dutch, had been impressed with such unfavorable opinions of the Russians. We had even entertained apprehensions lest our prisoners be put to death. Providence, however, watched over their safety, and their misfortune has effected what is almost unknown among humans, and we had made a vast step toward a future relationship. There are even grounds to hope that a further challenge for arbitration, advantageous for both nations, may take place between them.

Because I had reason to fear that our worn-out vessel might founder in the harbor of Petropaulowski, like the ship that had served in the expedition of Captain Billings, we ran her right ashore onto the beach. The *Diana*, no longer able to contend with the waves of the ocean, now serves as a magazine, and will be a memorial of former times.

It seems probable that these shores, celebrated by the voyages of Cook and La Perouse, and whose geographical situation is so advantageous for trade, will become better known to the neighboring Asiatic nations, and be visited by navigators from the most distant corners of the world. Then will the *Diana* perhaps often engage the attention of those who love to reflect on the wonderful course of human events.

On the day of our arrival at Petropaulowski all was cheerfulness in our little circle, with one exception. The unfortunate Moor alone presented a different aspect. His conduct arose from error, not from turpitude of heart or any settled design of treason to his country. Being bereft of all hope of returning to Russia and flattered with the idea of obtaining freedom among the Japanese, he was induced to depart from the path of honor.

When circumstances unexpectedly changed, he became every day more and more and more depressed in spirits, and finally yielded to despair. A man of ordinary mind might be easily brought to forget his own errors, but not one with a heart in which every honorable sentiment has been deeply rooted and was forever poisoned by a single offence.

When he first came on board the ship, after his liberation, I eagerly moved to embrace him, but he drew back, and reaching his sabre out to me, exclaimed, in a faltering voice, *"I am unworthy of your notice! I am only fit to be confined with criminals!"*

What a blow to a heart like mine, which had just been so completely transported with joy! I feared lest the seamen observe what was passing, and suddenly collecting myself, took the sabre, and said,

"I receive it as a memorial of this happy day."
I then conducted him to the cabin, where Captain Golownin and Mr. Chlebnikoff were expressing their gratitude to the officers of the vessel. Golownin presented his sabre to me. The same sabre that the Emperor of Japan had expressed a wish to see during the captain's captivity. I now preserve it as the most valuable reward of my enterprise.

To the officers Captain Golownin gave his telescope, pistols, and astronomical instruments. He gave to the senior non-commissioned officer one hundred rubles; to the juniors seventy-five; to each seaman twenty-five; and to the sailors who had been his companions in captivity, five hundred rubles each. To Makaroff who as the reader knows, he was of his particular importance to Captain Golownin while they were in captivity, he granted besides a pension, amounting to a seamen's annual pay, his estate in the territory of Casan.

To the Kurile, Alexei, he gave a set of carpenter's tools, a rifle, powder, shot, tobacco and two hundred and fifty rubles in cash. Even Moor took occasion to express his gratitude, but he constantly turned to me with the words, *"I am unworthy!"*

Golownin frequently entreated him to forget what had passed, as he had himself blotted it all from his recollection. Mr. Moor, however, was over-whelmed with remorse. The exhortations of friendship produced no effect upon him. He generally maintained a gloomy silence. The rest is known to the reader. Moor was a young man of extraordinary talent, and always distinguished himself in the performance of his duty.

To all the qualifications of a seaman, in their fullest extent, he added the knowledge of other sciences; was familiar with several foreign languages, and spoke two of them fluently. With such a character and such accomplishments it was impossible not to love him, and I am confident that all who knew him will participate in the sorrow of his old shipmates for the unhappy termination of his career.

FINIS.

Admiral Rikord's
letter to Japan
dated 1844

Въ заключеніе этой главы скажемъ нѣсколько словъ о послѣдующихъ дѣйствіяхъ Рикорда, имѣвшихъ отношеніе къ Японіи.

Въ 1844 году Рикордъ писалъ къ своимъ друзьямъ Японцамъ:

«Прошло 32 года, какъ я распрощался съ вами, почтенные Мура-Ками-Теске, Кумаджеро и вѣрный мой другъ *Таішо* (почетный титулъ Такатая-Кахи), въ Хакодате. Легко сказать: 32 года, но трудно прожить ихъ.— Мой другъ Головнинъ, котораго я не перестаю оплакивать, давно умеръ. Россія въ немъ лишилась весьма умнаго и добродѣтельнаго человѣка, а мы, друзья его, добраго друга. Но такъ Богу угодно: рано или поздно мы всѣ должны умереть, и по смерти переселиться, если были добры, кто бы ни были — Англичанинъ, Японецъ, Голландецъ, Русскій — въ ясное, чистое, свѣтлое Небо (Тэнъ); а если были злы — въ темное, какъ ночь, мѣсто. Сколько въ 32 года случилось въ свѣтѣ большихъ перемѣнъ, а я въ моей къ вамъ дружбѣ не измѣнился, и никогда не забуду, что вашимъ благороднымъ, дружескимъ стараніемъ имѣлъ я счастіе, при помощи Провидѣнія (Тэнъ), возвратить изъ Японіи моего друга Головнина.

«Въ доказательство, что Японія у меня всегда въ памяти, скажу вамъ, что по моему совѣту директоры торговой (Сѣверо-Американской) компаніи отвезли къ вамъ въ первый разъ, въ 1836 году, вашихъ людей на островъ Итурупъ, и прямо скажу вамъ, что я опечалился, узнавъ какъ съ берега палили изъ пушекъ по русскому судну. Судите теперь о моей радости, когда директоры той компаніи увѣдомили меня, что другіе 6 Японцевъ, также потерпѣвшіе, въ 1841 году, бѣдствіе, опять были отвезены, въ 1843 г., на тотъ же островъ и что на русское судно пріѣзжалъ Кавайосъ-Асалгаро и предлагалъ отъ начальника воду, дрова и провизію, и сказалъ, что русскія суда могутъ приходить въ Кунаширъ, Матсмай и Нипонъ для полученія провизіи, и что Японцы будутъ обходиться съ ними дружески.

«Благодарю Провидѣніе, что я дожилъ до такого счастливаго времени, когда умные и добрые Японцы вѣрятъ наконецъ, что мы, Русскіе — народъ мирный и ничего кромѣ дружбы и добраго согласія съ японскимъ государствомъ не желаемъ. Великій японскій мудрецъ, Кунятъ-Зе, сказалъ, что надобно любить своего ближняго. Кто къ вамъ ближе изъ всѣхъ европейскихъ государствъ, если не Россія, по разстоянію отъ земли вашей и по своимъ поступкамъ? Я сказалъ, что мы ближніе по поступкамъ, и вотъ это надобно пояснить. Слушайте (Ханасъ).

«Въ древнія времена, почти 2000 лѣтъ назадъ, нашъ святой человѣкъ говорилъ своимъ ученикамъ: тотъ истинно добродѣтеленъ, кто любитъ своего ближняго, какъ самъ себя. Одинъ изъ учениковъ спросилъ у него: «кто мой ближній»? Святой человѣкъ отвѣчалъ слѣдующею повѣстію: Бѣдный человѣкъ попался на дорогѣ къ разбойникамъ; они сняли съ него платье, изранили его и оставили едва живаго. По дорогѣ, гдѣ лежалъ бѣдный, израненый человѣкъ, шелъ священникъ (Бонза), посмотрѣлъ на него и прошелъ мимо; также шелъ большой чиновникъ (Буніосъ), подошелъ, посмотрѣлъ на него, и прошелъ мимо; а простой человѣкъ шелъ за ними, увидѣлъ бѣднаго, сжалился надъ нимъ, перевязалъ его раны, привелъ его въ свой домъ, кормилъ и лечилъ его, пока онъ выздоровѣлъ. Святой человѣкъ потомъ спросилъ ученика: кто былъ ближній бѣдному, попавшему къ разбойникамъ? Ученикъ отвѣчалъ: тотъ, кто оказалъ ему милость. Тогда святой человѣкъ сказалъ: поди, и дѣлай такъ, какъ дѣлалъ этотъ бѣдный,—и съ тѣхъ поръ всѣ добрые люди исполняютъ то, что сказалъ святой человѣкъ. Если вы также думаете, то разсудите сами: Японія и Россія два большія государства; унихъ все есть для человѣческой жизни, они ни въ чемъ не нуждаются, но согласитесь, что не хорошо и грѣшно вамъ не имѣть съ нами, вашими сосѣдями, дружескаго сношенія

«Какъ желалъ бы я еще разъ съ вами повидаться и обо всемъ этомъ съ вами поговорить, хотя теперь я уже старый человѣкъ, но, благодаря Бога, здоровъ и море . . для меня не страшно. Съ тѣхъ поръ какъ я съ вами рас- . .рощался, много плавалъ я по всѣмъ морямъ, какъ глав-ный начальникъ нашихъ большихъ военныхъ кораблей. Посылаю вамъ въ память дружбы мои портреты; прошу принять ихъ не подаркомъ, а въ видѣ другаго письма, только не перомъ, а рѣзцомъ написаннаго. Будьте здоро-вы, во всемъ благополучны и долгоденственны, добрые друзья мои, и вѣрьте, что всегда помнитъ и любитъ васъ другъ вашъ П. Рикордъ».

Въ отвѣтъ на это письмо Рикордъ получилъ, при столь же дружескомъ посланіи, парадный японскій «мун-диръ», въ которомъ и изображенъ на портретѣ, бывшемъ на выставкѣ Академіи, въ 1854 году. Въ этомъ нарядѣ принималъ Рикордъ близкихъ своихъ знакомыхъ, и съ обычною веселостью объяснялъ имъ удобства японска- «мундира». — «Широкіе рукава, говорилъ Петръ Ива-новичъ, служатъ канцеляріей для японскаго чиновника; въ нихъ онъ кладетъ бумаги, чернилицу, кисть, которою пишетъ, и другія принадлежности письмоводства; въ ру-кава же прячетъ и ту бумагу, которая служитъ вмѣсто нашихъ носовыхъ платковъ, и которую Японцы, разъ употребивъ въ дѣло, бросаютъ. Видя, что мы не бросаемъ своихъ носовыхъ платковъ, а прячемъ ихъ, послѣ кажда-го употребленія, въ карманы, Японцы говорили: охота же вамъ носить въ карманѣ такую дрянь»!

Японія и Камчатка были любимою тэмою разгово-ровъ Петра Ивановича; въ квартирѣ его все напоминало

Respectful Murakami-Teisuke, Kumajiro, and my sincere friend Taisho,

Thirty-two years have flown since our farewell at Hakodate and it has been very difficult to live those years, and they are not easy to describe in words.

Also, it has been quite some time since my dear friend Golownin passed away but I still do not stop praying for him and I miss him a lot. It was a great loss for Russia and his friends losing wise and noble man like Golownin.

It may be God's will to fade away soon or later. That is the same with English, Japanese, Dutch, and Russians, whatever our country may be. We must relocate to the clear and bright heaven. A man of evil must relocate to the darkness of night.

Even though I have encountered numerous changes I never experienced ones similar to those thirty-two years. Yet, my friendship with every one of you has never faded and I never forget that I was fortunate to release Golownin, who is now in the heaven, and bring him home from Japan with your generosity and friendship.

I was also fortunate that I could live long enough to

see wise and good Japanese people finally in belief that the Russian nation respects peace and no desire for aggression. It desires no more than a good neighborhood and agreement among its neighbors. One Japanese wise man says that the Japanese people have to share affection with neighboring countries. Distance between two countries and mutual conduct are closer than any other countries in Europe. I wish to mention this based on our mutual conduct code.

We should listen and speak to each other very carefully. Japan and Russia are two big powers. These two countries have most everything people need to live and no shortages. Yet, I wish you to agree that it is no good not having good relationship and it is rather a sin. I am already quite old but I wish to meet you once again and talk about the old days. I am still in good health and I do not fear navigation over the sea. Even after the farewell with all of you, I led a number of fleets as a commander crossing numerous oceans.

I wish for the happiness of every one of you, and of my good friends and neighbors. Please know in your heart that your friend P. Rikord remembers every one of you and loves you all.

In the year 1844

Episode 1:

Commodore M.C. Perry (1794-1858) of the U.S. Navy visited Hakodate in 1854 on his second expedition. He was well acquainted with Japan and about the people prior to his arrival in Japan partially through this history.

Commodore Perry's arrival
at Hakodate in 1854

Several years later, coincidently both U.S. and Japan fought respective civil war at around the same time. Tokugawa Bakufu Regime ended in 1867 and new Meiji restoration was started in 1868 that was only three years after the U.S. Civil War ended in 1865.

Hokuidan

Russian ship
in Hakodate

Hakodate
Central Library
函館中央図書館

Episode 2:

Nicholas of Japan (1836-1912) Dimitry Kasatkin was also fascinated by this story. He arrived at Hakodate in 1861, as a missionary for the church of the Russian Consulate in Hakodate. Later he moved to Tokyo where he built another church called, "Nikorai Doh" that stands at one side of the Kanda river on top of the bank called "Kanda Suruga Dai," where Tokugawa Bakufu astronomy and land survey ministry (Ten Mon Kata) 天文方 was also once located. Nicholas spent rest of his life in Japan, reflecting P. I. Rikord's belief.

On the other side of the valley Nicholas witnessed changes of Japanese history and a sacred temple, called "Yushima Sei Doh" 湯島聖堂, a national temple of the Confucianism and a birthplace of culture and education, core spirit of "Bushi Do" 武士道. This place is now referred to as a birthplace of Ministry of Education and Science, including the University of Tokyo 東京大学 (昌平坂学問所) and its annexed medical institute, as well as men's and also women's teachers colleges.

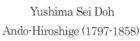

Yushima Sei Doh
Ando-Hiroshige (1797-1858)

Underline References:

(*): Notation made for this edition.

(**): Notation made in 1824 translation

		The First Voyage
P7	*	Eleventh month: It implies, "silence before storm" and it also represents right before things are about to complete by referring one year completes in 12 months.
	*	Ancient calendar: The Julian calendar declared by Peter the Great starts from September.
	*	_Diana_: Sloop type battleship built in England
	*	Captain: Equivalent of today's Lieutenant Commander of the U.S. Navy
	*	Kamchatka: See Map (A) Peninsula; Spelled (Kamschatka) in 1824 translation
P8	*	Japanese history: Christians were persecuted as a prohibited religion.
P9	*	Two fathoms and half: about 4.57m (15 ft.) One fathom is about 1.83m (6 ft.)
P10	*	Kunashiri: 国後島 See Map (A) Spelled (Kunashier) in 1824 translation
P11	*	Okhotsk: See Map (B) Spelled (Okhotzk) in 1824 translation
	*	The second pilot: The second navigator
P12	*	Baidare(s): Local small boat

	*	Midshipman: Rank of Imperial Russian Navy, equivalent to the current U.S. Navy Ensign
P15	*	Irkutzk:　See Map (B)
P16	*	Jakutzk:　See Map (B)
	*	Three thousand wersts: 3,200 km (2,000 miles) One werst is about 1.067km (0.663miles)
	*	Forty-five wersts: about 48 km (30 miles)
P18	*	Leonsaimon: 良左衛門 Name of Japanese drifted in the sea Spelled (Leonsaimo) in 1824 translation
P19	*	Tungusians: Native people or tribes, widely spread around Siberia and into northern China
P21	**	Pikoff Channel:　Kunashiri Suidou 国後水道 See Map (A)
	*	Strait of Defries:　Etorofu Kaikyo 択捉海峡 See Map (A)
P22	*	Twenty fathoms:　about 37m (40 yards)
P24	*	Urup Island: 得撫島　See Map (A) Spelled (Ooroopa) in 1824 translation.
	*	Etorofu: 択捉島　See Map (A) Spelled (Eetooroopa) in 1824 translation.
	*	Shikotan: 色丹島　See Map (A) Spelled (Tshikotana) in 1824 translation.
P35	*	Matsumae: 松前　See Map (A) Spelled (Matsmai) in 1824 translation.
	*	Nagasaki: 長崎　See Map (B)

		Spelled (Nangasaky) in 1824 translation.
	*	Edo: 江戸 See Map (B) Japanese capital city, renamed as Tokyo; after Meiji restoration Spelled (Yeddo) in 1824 translation.
P39	*	Takataya-Kahei: 高田屋嘉兵衛 Spelled (Takatay-Kachi) in 1824 translation
	*	Sendo-Funamochi: 船頭船持 Ship commander Spelled (Sindofnamotsh) in 1824 translation
	*	Hakodate: 函館 See Map (A) Spelled (Chakodade) in 1824 translation.
P48	*	Russian Vodka: described (Russian brandy) in 1824 translation
P49	*	Seven leagues: about 33.6km (21 miles) One league is about 4.8km (3 miles)
P52	*	Gorogee: 五郎次 Japanese who drifted in the sea. Spelled (Chorodsee) in 1824 translation
	*	Oyakata: 親方 a chief or a leader. Spelled (Oyagodo) in 1824 translation
	*	Nambu: 南部(藩) Territorial or clan name, currently part of Iwate and Aomori prefectures.
P53	*	La Bussole Strait: See Map (A)
	*	Raikoke: See Map (A)
	*	Matua: See Map (A)
P54	*	Awatscha: See Map (A)
	*	Petrepaulowski: See Map (A)
	*	Kanton: 広東 (currently Guangzhou 廣州)

		Name of the city in China
		The Second Voyage
P59	*	<u>bugyo</u>: 奉行 office or a person who carry out judicial issues and recognized as governor in 1824 translation and spelled (bunyo).
P67	*	<u>Hara-Kiri</u>: 切腹 was considered being honorable death to crucify himself by cutting his berry.
P72	*	<u>Fushigi!</u>： 不思議　wonder, mystery, strange Spelled (Fissingi!) in 1824 translation
P82	*	<u>Takahashi-Sampei</u>: 高橋三平;　Spelled (Takahassy-Sampey) in 1824 translation
P85	*	<u>Kujimoto-Hyogoro</u>: 柑本兵五郎;　Spelled (Cood-Simoto- Chiogoro) in 1824 translation
		The Third Voyage
P94	*	<u>Vulcano Bay</u>: 噴火湾（内浦湾）Map (A) Large circle bay located at upper north of Hakodate.
	*	<u>Etomo</u>: 絵鞆　Map (A)　Located at east rim of the Vulcano Bay.
	*	<u>Sandwich Islands</u>:　Captain James Cook gave this name to today's Hawaiian Islands in 1770s.
P96	*	<u>Sawara</u>: 砂原 Located at south rim of Vulcano Bay.　Spelled (SANGARO) in 1824 translation
P97	*	<u>Ainu</u>: アイヌ called Kuriles as well. Spelled (Ainos) in 1824 translation
	*	<u>Heizo</u>: 平蔵　Spelled (Leso) in 1824 translation

P99	*	<u>Yamase-Tomari</u>: 山背泊 anchoring point Spelled (Yamasee-Tomuree) in 1824 translation
	*	<u>Hattori-Bingono-kami</u>: 服部備後守; Spelled (Chattori-Bingono-Kami) in 1824 translation
P100	*	French, Napoleon Bonaparte, invasion of Russia in 1812
P104	**	<u>White flag</u> : *I ought to have mentioned, that the white flag was constantly displayed along with the flag of war.*
P116	*	<u>Murakami-Teisuke</u>: 村上貞助 Spelled (Murakami-Teske) in 1824 translation
P123	*	<u>lantern</u>: 提灯
	**	*He alluded to the story of Diogenes, which Rikord related to Kahei in Kamchatka, and he was highly pleased. In general he was deeply interested by the examples of virtue and greatness of soul, such as the conduct of the celebrated Dolgoruki, when he tore the order of Peter the Great. Whenever he listened to that anecdote he would place his hand on his head in gesture of veneration, and exclaim with emotion,* *"Okee!, Okee!" (Great! Great!) Then pressing his hand to his heart he would say, Kusuri ! (medicine!) A term by which he was accustomed to designate any dish that particularly pleased him, and of which to express his admiration.*

P126	*	hashi: 箸 Two pieces of wooden sticks used instead of folks (Chasees) in 1824 translation
	*	sakazuki: 杯 Small cup in which sake is served.
	**	Lacquered cups and small pieces of wood, which the Japanese use instead of knives and forks.
P128	*	Ginmiyaku: 吟味役 Rank of Japanese officials Spelled (Ginmiyaks) in 1824 translation
P130	*	Vodka: (Brandy) in 1824 translation
	*	Sake: 酒 Japanese rice wine
	*	Shitayaku: 下役 rank of Japanese officials Spelled (Shtoyagu) in 1824 translation
	*	Zaiju-Kumajiro: 在住熊次郎 (Saidshu-Kumaddschero) in 1824 translation